creating
success

J3

Taking
Minutes of
Meetings

CREATING SUCCESS

With over 1 million copies sold in over 30 languages, the Creating Success series covers 13 key skills and features bestselling authors Michael Armstrong and John Adair.

@KPEmployability

www.koganpage.com/creating-success

creating
success

Taking
Minutes of
Meetings

Joanna
Gutmann

KoganPage

First published in Great Britain and the United States in 2001 by Kogan Page Limited
Second edition 2006
Third edition 2013
Fourth edition 2016

2nd Floor, 45 Gee Street	122 W 27th St	4737/23 Ansari Road
London	10th Floor	Daryaganj
EC1V 3RS	New York NY 10001	New Delhi 110002
United Kingdom	USA	India

© Joanna Gutmann, 2001, 2006, 2013, 2016

The right of Joanna Gutmann to be identified as the author of this work has been asserted by her in accordance with the Copyright, Designs and Patents Act 1988.

ISBN 978 0 7494 7579 6
E-ISBN 978 0 7494 7580 2

British Library Cataloguing-in-Publication Data

A CIP record for this book is available from the British Library.

Library of Congress Cataloging-in-Publication Data

Names: Gutmann, Joanna, author.
Title: Taking minutes of meetings / Joanna Gutmann.
Description: Fourth edition. | New York, NY : Kogan Page, 2016. | Series: Creating success | Revised edition of the author's Taking minutes of meetings, 2013.
Identifiers: LCCN 2016031318 (print) | LCCN 2016039459 (ebook) | ISBN 9780749475796 (paperback) | ISBN 9780749475802 (ebook)
Subjects: LCSH: Business meetings. | Business communication. | Corporate minutes. | Business records. | BISAC: BUSINESS & ECONOMICS / Careers / General. | BUSINESS & ECONOMICS / Secretarial Aids & Training. | BUSINESS & ECONOMICS / Business Communication / Meetings & Presentations. | SELF-HELP / Personal Growth / General.
Classification: LCC HF5734.5 .G88 2016 (print) | LCC HF5734.5 (ebook) | DDC 651.7/7–dc23
LC record available at https://lccn.loc.gov/2016031318

Typeset by Graphicraft Limited, Hong Kong
Print production managed by Jellyfish
Printed and bound by CPI Group (UK) Ltd, Croydon CR0 4YY

Contents

Introduction

Minutes are vital to the success of the meeting. Participants rely on them for information on subjects they did not understand or to fill in gaps when they lost concentration. The action points act as a reminder to those who agreed in the heat of the moment but have since been overtaken by other priorities and would otherwise forget what they were to do. Those who could not attend need an idea of what was decided in their absence. Minutes are also the historical record of the meeting and evidence of the outcomes and actions. At some stage in the future, when the participants have probably moved on (and almost certainly forgotten what happened at the meeting), an investigation may be held in the light of a negative event. The minutes are the only record of what decisions were made and why, together with how they were implemented.

Particularly in the public sector, there is increasing pressure of 'governance', and it is vital that, at any time in the near or distant future, an outsider can see from the minutes what was decided, the action that was to be taken to make that decision happen, and the later confirmation that the action was taken – the 'audit trail'.

For a role that carries significant responsibility, there is very little support for the minute-taker. There is a common misconception that secretaries can take minutes. This seems to stem from two sources: first, the word 'secretary' as in committee secretary; secondly, the idea that taking minutes is about speed and secretaries can write fast, particularly if they have shorthand. This perception broadens to anyone in an administrative role.

In fact, a secretary is only a little more likely to be trained to take minutes than to be a company secretary. The perception that minute taking is all about speed is also wrong. Ask someone what they are copy-typing and they are likely to stop and look at it before answering – typing does not involve the brain on a conscious level; shorthand is similar. Speed is only achieved when the brain isn't needed because the body is using a learned 'mechanical' skill. Whilst fast, legible writing is an advantage for minute-takers, what is needed is a combination of good listening skills and confidence to clarify where necessary.

The key skill for taking minutes is the ability to listen to the words someone is saying, absorb them, evaluate the manner of the delivery and identify the speaker's point of view – the message. It is ongoing listening and simultaneous summarizing. Although a good shorthand writer can take down the words and summarize them back in the office, it is a long drawn-out process and few can afford the time.

Assuming that the minute-taker gets involved in the setting up of the meeting, as many do, there is also the need for good administration skills, particularly in today's world where meetings are often rescheduled, rooms are in short supply, budgets are being cut and time is at a premium for all concerned.

There is a second type of minute-taker: people who attend to contribute but find themselves taking the notes in the absence of administrative support. Although they have the advantages of higher status within the group and a better understanding, they also suffer from the problems of identifying what is relevant and how to note it effectively. They also find it harder to remain objective as, by definition, they have an interest in the content. In addition, they may not be trained typists and thus find presenting the minutes in a professional style difficult.

The people who attend my courses have a range of problems with the role, mainly to do with the issue of what to write or coping

in a badly led meeting. Quite a few report sleepless nights before a meeting and feelings of stress before, during and after it. Few have received any training, and although many have been taking minutes for years, the lack of clear focus and structure for the meetings has made them wonder about the 'theory' behind the practice.

Today, meetings are far less structured than in the past and it is generally felt that there are many more of them, probably far too many. Very few people believe this to be a good thing; the time taken (and often wasted) by meetings is resented by those who attend as well as by those who minute. Meetings that are well run are appreciated by everyone, and the minute-taker plays a large part in achieving this. Although it is the chairperson who 'fronts' and controls the meeting, it is the support of the minute-taker that enables this to be done effectively.

In most organizations, there are no 'rules' for minutes: some want formality, others a more casual style; some want all the detail, others only a list of action points. Any guidance is usually limited to house style for layout, not content. The minute-taker has to be flexible and responsive to the needs of both the chairperson and the group.

The minute-taker is one of the most important and powerful people in a meeting. Although the task can be daunting, it is the opportunity to develop your knowledge, broaden your horizons, network and build your credibility within the organization. With a clear idea of your role and responsibilities, knowledge of what you are meant to do and some confidence in yourself, your role as minute-taker can even be enjoyable!

Using the book

The book is intended to be used as a reference book. It follows the cycle of a meeting from the decision to hold one through to the dispatch of the minutes. You can read it from cover to cover or dip

in to find the help you need on any given aspect of the minute-taker's role.

It is assumed that you have little or no knowledge of the 'theory' of minute taking, although you may have plenty of experience. The book is laid out with lots of headings and with short paragraphs. This will help you to skip the information you already know or don't need for your meetings, and focus on the detail you want.

Terms

A number of terms are used throughout the book as I've tried to avoid repetition, and these may mean different things to different people. The following explains my meanings:

- *Meeting*. An event involving a group of people, getting together to discuss and/or decide. This might be a board meeting, a committee or sub-committee, a team or other informal meeting, a one-off or ad hoc meeting, or a panel (eg disciplinary). It could also be a contract or supplier/provider meeting or a one-to-one complaint discussion.

- *Committee*. The group of people who are meeting, even though it may not be a formally constituted committee. I've also used the terms group, team, members, etc.

- *Chairperson*. The person who is leading the meeting. Could also be a facilitator, mediator, convener.

- *Secretary/minute-taker*. The person who is responsible for the administration of the meeting: setting it up, preparing the agenda, dealing with the room booking, coffee, etc, taking the minutes and so on. Although I've used the two titles at random through-out the book, some will argue that a secretary does all the tasks above, while a minute-taker's role is limited to taking notes, typing them up and distributing them. Throughout the book, I've assumed that you are responsible for all aspects of the

administration – just ignore the bits that don't apply to your work.

There is a lot information in the book about your role and responsibilities and the importance of every aspect of doing the job professionally to create good minutes that will meet the needs of users now and in the future. However, don't lose sight of the fact that you are working with humans in an office setting and a good dose of humour and friendly self-confidence is an invaluable weapon in the minute-taker's armoury.

1 Background

Business meetings fall into one of two broad categories – the regular and the one-off. They are generally held to spread information, to discuss issues, to solve problems and/or to decide on future action. In addition there are the panel meetings, those that investigate HR issues such as disciplinary and grievance or safeguarding issues relating to the care of a child or vulnerable person. Finally there are the short-notice meetings, which are often felt to not need minutes but where a confirmation e-mail or file-note would be useful.

A meeting can be a positive or negative experience, depending on the skill of the chairperson and the attitude of those attending. The most common complaints from those who attend are:

- Participants couldn't have their say.
- Discussion degenerated into argument.
- The meeting was dominated by one or two 'loud voices'.
- The chairperson took over.
- The chairperson did nothing to control the meeting.
- Irrelevant discussion was allowed.
- Nothing was decided.
- It was generally a waste of time (and often stressful through anger and frustration).

From the minute-taker's point of view, the first of the above complaints is not relevant, but the others are. A meeting that is badly

> Add up the annual salaries of those attending £
> Add 25% on-cost + 25% = £
> Divide by 52 (weeks of the year) ÷ 52 = £
> Divide by standard hours per ÷ 37 = £ = cost per
> week (eg 37) hour
> Multiply by time of meeting
> (eg 2 hours) × 2 = £
> Add in any costs of room hire,
> refreshments + £ = £ = cost of
> meeting
>
> Using this calculation, eight people earning £30,000 per annum,
> meeting for two hours, will cost the organization around £325. Is it
> worth it?

FIGURE 1.1 Calculating the cost of a meeting

structured and uncontrolled will definitely be stressful and frustrating and will waste far more time than just the allotted span. The time taken in sorting the notes and typing up the minutes can add hours to the workload.

On the basis that 'time is money', meetings are expensive. Try the exercise in Figure 1.1 for one of your meetings.

There is far more to the meeting than just the time spent around the table. In order to be successful, everybody must:

- know why they are there;
- recognize what is to be achieved;
- have read all paperwork in advance;
- be prepared (mental and practical preparation);
- contribute positively;
- listen;
- focus and keep to the point;
- accept the final group decision;
- leave with a clear understanding of any points they should action.

The minute-taker has a role to play in several of the points above – like so many things, good preparation will make for a good meeting. The agenda should give information as to the purpose of every item, the structure the meeting will follow and the preparation that needs to be done. It must be dispatched in time for this to be useful. The minutes will show the reasons why decisions were reached, what those decisions were and the individual action points that will make them a reality. They also act as an audit trail to demonstrate that those actions have been taken, and if not, what is to be done about them.

The regular meeting

Cycle of the meeting

The cycle shown in Figure 1.2 assumes a monthly meeting, held on the 1st of each month. The bracketed number indicates the target date for each action.

For less frequent meetings, the principle of agenda dispatched a week before, minutes despatched within a week should still hold. For weekly meetings, the dates generally change from a week to a couple of days.

For many people, the cycle of the meeting will seem to set impossibly tight deadlines, but:

• If you do not like typing up your minutes, they only get worse with procrastination.

• If you are going to have to ring and ask a participant for guidance on the content, it is better to do it whilst he or she can remember what was said.

• If the minutes are not circulated quickly, the action points are a waste of time; it will be too late for participants to take action.

• You look inefficient if the minutes are not circulated until the next month's meeting.

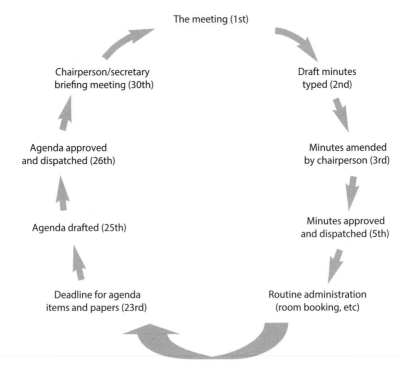

FIGURE 1.2 Cycle of a meeting

THE STAGES IN THE CYCLE

- *First draft of minutes*
 (one day after the meeting)
 The first draft should be the minutes, typed as the minute-taker perceives the discussion. They may well contain gaps where the chairperson's guidance is needed, but should be as near complete as possible.

- *Chairperson's approval*
 (two to three days after meeting)
 The chairperson should check the minutes for factual accuracy and 'political correctness' – phrasing that may cause offence or

that does not represent the view of the group. The chairperson should not add any extra information or change the minutes to suit personal views.

- *Minutes dispatched*
 (five days after meeting)
 The minutes should be sent to all committee members and anyone else who gets a copy. Any papers that were distributed at the meeting should be attached for those who did not attend.

- *Routine administration*
 The booking of rooms, coffee, etc usually falls to the minute-taker. Throughout the book you'll find advice and guidance on improving the meeting's effectiveness through these routine tasks.

- *Deadline for agenda items*
 (around eight days before next meeting)
 Under 'Date of next meeting' in the minutes, a deadline for agenda items should have been given (see Chapter 11). Anything that is received after this can be dealt with under 'Any other business'. All papers for discussion at the meeting must be submitted by this date so they can be included with the agenda. In reality, the secretary is usually left to ring or e-mail to nag participants for agenda items and papers.

- *Draft agenda*
 (seven days before next meeting)
 The secretary should put together the agenda and pass it to the chairperson for approval.

- *Agenda dispatched*
 (one week before next meeting)
 Each participant should receive an agenda and all papers that are to be discussed. The agenda should be cross-referenced to indicate which papers relate to each agenda item. Hints as to other preparation may be included (see Chapter 4).

- *Briefing*
 (one to two days before next meeting)
 The chairperson and minute-taker should meet to discuss the
 content of the meeting, identify any problem areas and deal with
 any concerns either party has about the meeting. This is seldom
 a formal event, but is often a brief chat before, or on the way to,
 the meeting. The formality will be influenced by the style of the
 people involved and the importance of the meeting.
- *The meeting*
 If the rest of the cycle of the meeting is in place, the event itself
 should be efficient and successful.

The participants

There are four roles in a meeting: to lead it (chairperson), to support
it (secretary), to contribute to it or to observe it. Only one person
can take each of the first two roles, but they are closely interlinked
– the management of the meeting shared by two people. Any number
can attend or observe.

The participants are responsible for a certain amount of work
before, during and after the meeting.

THE CHAIRPERSON

Before the meeting:

- Decide that the meeting is necessary.
- Identify participants (who needs to attend all/just part of the
 meeting).
- Approve the agenda.
- Brief the minute-taker.
- Prepare self (content, purpose of each item, participants, where
 actions are necessary).

During the meeting:

- Introduce newcomers and visitors.
- Inform the delegates of the agreed behaviours (eg how decisions will be reached).
- Control the agenda (content, time, order and outcomes).
- Control delegate contributions.
- Work with and support the minute-taker.

After the meeting:

- Approve the minutes within three days of the meeting.
- Collect and assess any feedback.
- Support participants with their action points where necessary.

THE MINUTE-TAKER

The role of the minute-taker varies immensely from one group to the next. Some just want the minimum: take the notes and type them into a first draft of minutes. Others want full administrative support, even going as far as guiding the chairperson during the meeting.

Before the meeting:

- Set up the meeting (advise of date, room booking, refreshments, etc).
- Ensure that everyone knows where and when to attend.
- Prepare a detailed agenda.
- Ensure distribution of information (to participants, and others if necessary).
- Prepare self (read papers and previous minutes, familiarize with names, etc).

During the meeting:

- Take the minutes.

After the meeting:

- Approach the chairperson or participants to clarify any misunderstandings.
- Type up the minutes within a couple of days.
- Ensure the minutes are approved and dispatched.

THOSE ATTENDING THE MEETING

Contributors

Before the meeting:

- Request a meeting if necessary.
- Respond quickly to the invitation to the meeting.
- Send items for the agenda in good time.
- Read the agenda and accompanying papers.
- Ensure that previous actions are complete.

During the meeting:

- Arrive on time and prepared.
- Contribute appropriately (as to both time and manner).
- Keep contributions relevant to the agenda.
- Show common courtesy and respect for others' opinions.
- Note personal action points.

After the meeting:

- Complete action points within deadlines agreed.
- Read and respond to minutes.

Observers

Before the meeting:

- Ensure their purpose for attending is clear.
- Undertake any necessary preparation.

During the meeting:

- Observe, but don't contribute.

After the meeting:

- Write up any necessary notes.
- If appropriate, give feedback to the chairperson.

If all the participants are aware of what they have to achieve and are well briefed, and the chairperson is focused and effective, the minute-taker's task should not be difficult.

Who will use the minutes

For most meetings there are four groups of people who may have an interest in reading the minutes:

- The meeting participants, to remind themselves of what was discussed or, more commonly, to find out what they agreed to do.
- Other interested parties, particularly if they are published on the internet.
- An investigator in the future who is tasked with finding out what went wrong regarding an issue, and who may be unable to contact those who made decisions or are able to remember what happened at the time.
- A more benign future user who can remember that 'we did this before', and again has only the minutes to give information on what was done and how.

The one-off meeting

These are often the informal meetings held at short notice in response to an issue arising that needs the 'team to get together' to discuss. They may be the everyday buyer/supplier type or the general update type. These are often seen as not needing minutes but, in fact, benefit from an e-mail to summarize what was discussed and confirm the outcome, or at least a file note for future reference. There are also the panel meetings, such as an HR disciplinary, grievance or serious incident investigation.

The informal meetings are often held at short notice so it may not be possible to produce an agenda in advance; if this is the case, the meeting should start with clarification of what will be covered and this will form the structure for the minutes. It is worth ensuring that there is an administrative system in place so that in the future it is clear whether actions were taken.

Panel meetings should follow a much clearer structure, much closer to the business meeting than may be apparent at first. There may be a separate system for recording outcomes and actions. The chairperson should take a more directive role and may not use an agenda in a recognized format; the minutes generally follow a set structure.

(See Chapter 14 for guidance on minuting these types of meetings.)

Responsibility for the minutes

The role of minute-taker is a 'delegated task' from the chairperson. The management of the meeting is divided into people and content management (chairperson) and admin/note-taking (minute-taker). The process should be:

- The minute-taker is responsible for taking notes in the meeting. That means that he or she either understands and writes, or asks for clarification where it is needed. (Note: you are not responsible for knowing and understanding everything that every participant knows!)

- The minute-taker should prepare draft minutes to the best of their ability (using their notes and asking for clarification where necessary).

- The chairperson should approve the draft before it is sent out. This means that, although the minute-taker will still be doing the work or amendments and despatch, the responsibility for the content has moved to the chairperson.

- The group should approve the minutes at the next meeting. At this point the minutes become their responsibility (not the minute-taker's).

SUMMARY POINTS

- Meetings fall into the categories of:
 - regular;
 - one-off;
 - short notice (usually to deal with an immediate issue);
 - panel (often HR or social care based).

- The agenda should provide the participants with all the information they need to have an informed discussion and the chair with the support to manage that discussion and guide it to clear outcomes.

- The chair is responsible for managing the people, the content, the outcomes and the time.

- The participants are responsible for preparing well and contributing respectfully and productively.

- The minute-taker is responsible for getting the information needed for the minutes, summarizing discussion and ensuring a clear understanding of the decisions and actions.

2 Arranging a meeting

In theory, setting up a meeting should present no problem: a few e-mails or phone calls, a confirmation diary/schedule note or e-mail and that's it. Anyone who has tried to do it knows the reality: endless attempts to find mutually convenient dates, difficulty in booking rooms, and economies that mean no sandwiches and grumbling participants.

Keep an accurate and well-planned database of those who attend the meetings you set up. Since many will attend more than one meeting, it is generally best to keep one overall meeting database, rather than one for each meeting. This is typically done in Microsoft Access or Excel.

Use separate fields of first and surname (for ease of inserting the greeting), whatever contact details are necessary, and fields for job title and department (for merging into the minutes under 'Present', etc). Keep one field for a code to identify which meetings people attend; for example HS for Health and Safety, BP for Business Planning. Multiple codes can be entered for those who attend more than one meeting.

It is worth having one field called something like 'Mark'. This can be used for one-off meetings; just insert a familiar symbol in this field for everyone who is to attend and then use it to merge.

Merge with this database for address labels, circulation lists, attendance list on minutes and any other documents. Set up contact groups in e-mail for each meeting; this speeds up the sending of e-mails and ensures that no one is accidentally left off the circulation list.

Who will attend?

Before you begin, make sure you know who must attend, who should attend and what is needed for the meeting. You may be able to find some of this from previous minutes, but it is always best to speak to the chairperson to ensure you have all the information before you start making arrangements.

The regular meeting

For many meetings the dates are set at the beginning of the year. This is much the easiest way to approach it because it avoids taking time negotiating dates at the end of each meeting. It also helps the minute-taker as administration can be structured and entered in the diary or scheduler.

If this is not done, the date of the next meeting should be arranged as the final item on the previous agenda. It may be worth reminding people to bring their diaries or a note of their availability to the meeting. If necessary, prompt the chairperson to finish off each meeting by deciding when and where the next should be held. If this is forgotten in the rush to get out of the room, it is quite acceptable for the minute-taker to ask for the next date 'for the minutes'.

If the date of the meeting is not set, or if it has to be changed, find out whose attendance is essential: that is, their withdrawal would cause the meeting to be cancelled. These are the people with whom you should agree the date. The other participants can be

offered dates at the same time (with less priority given to their choice) or simply told of the date afterwards. It is not necessary to tell them that their importance is secondary and that they have to put up with the date!

It may be that some people are essential for only some of the items to be discussed. If this is the case, these items could be deferred to the next meeting if the relevant individuals cannot attend.

VISITORS

For many meetings there will be visitors who need to be invited on a one-off basis. These might be from other organizations or fellow employees, but they are not part of the group that meets regularly. Make sure you know whether visitors are needed for the whole meeting or just part of it. Make sure that visitors know:

- why they are attending;
- what will be asked of them;
- where their involvement fits into the overall objective of the meeting;
- who else will be present.

The one-off meeting

Before you begin to arrange the meeting find out who the 'priority people' are – those without whom the meeting cannot go ahead. If booking a room is likely to cause problems, this is also the time to check availability and reserve the room. Select a few dates, spreading them across different days of the week and times of the day and then e-mail everyone with a 'notice of meeting', explaining why the meeting is being held and offering dates. You might also wish to insert a personal sentence explaining why each individual's attendance is requested. Make sure that you give a clear deadline for confirming attendance. Figure 2.1 gives an example e-mail

From <dlatimer@mkthompson.co.uk.>
To: <wsmith@mkthompson.co.uk>
Sent: 10 March 2017 15:23
Subject: Resurfacing of car park

Notice of meeting

Alchemist Tarmac has gone into liquidation. We need to get together to decide what action to take and to start the process of selecting a new contractor from the tender list. I would anticipate that the meeting will last 45 minutes.

Please advise which of the following dates you are able to make:

Wednesday 22 March, 9.30 am
Wednesday 22 March, 3.00 pm
Thursday 23 March, 11.00 am
Monday 27 March, 10.30 am

Please reply by 11.00 am, Monday 13 March, and the meeting date will be confirmed by 3.00 pm that same day.

David

FIGURE 2.1 Example e-mail notice of meeting

notice of meeting. Note that the e-mail heading is the subject of the meeting, not 'Notice of meeting', so readers can immediately see what it is about.

Administration

Give due warning

If too little notice is given, participants will be ill-prepared. If papers have not been read, this will have to be done at the meeting. This not only wastes time, but comprehension is likely to be poor and readers often latch on to a point they strongly agree or disagree with. This leads to argument. If issues have not been thought through, arguing is again likely, as is a resultant poor decision.

If items are not fully discussed, or decisions are poor, the subject is likely to be raised again at the next meeting. This might be intentionally via the agenda or unintentionally because someone goes back to the subject. Inevitably the whole thing is discussed again, wasting considerable time.

There is no fixed rule for the amount of notice you should give, but ensure that it is enough for all preparation to be done, usually 5–7 days.

Get agenda items

For a one-off meeting, the notice of meeting should ask for agenda items and give a deadline for their receipt. Anything arising after that time will be dealt with as 'Any other business'.

For regular meetings, include a deadline for agenda items under 'Date of next meeting'. Throughout the meeting, listen for items that are left with a vague, 'We'll talk about that next time', because they will need to appear on the agenda. Some agenda items will follow naturally from previous meetings and the minute-taker will need to keep track of these.

Although it should not be necessary, the minute-taker will often have to ring around, asking for items. This can be lessened by asking the chairperson to finish the next meeting by explaining the deadline and pointing out that anything received after that date won't be accepted for the agenda. Providing that the rule is enforced, participants soon get the idea that laziness won't be tolerated. Items that can be shown to have arisen after the agenda was sent out can be taken as 'Any other business' as usual.

Allow sufficient time

Few people like long meetings, and the length of time taken is a common complaint. This is sometimes the fault of the chairperson for allowing non-productive argument and not drawing items to a close, and is sometimes caused by having an unrealistic number of items for discussion.

A meeting must be long enough to allow the business to be discussed completely. When items are sent in for the agenda, ask how long is required and use this to calculate the time necessary. This has the added advantage of developing your understanding of the issues through talking to participants, which will help when taking the minutes. If there is too much to be discussed in the time available, a second meeting should be arranged or some items deferred to the following meeting. This will have to be discussed with the chairperson.

There is no maximum time for a meeting, but one lasting for more than a couple of hours is bound to have periods when concentration slips. If the meeting is scheduled to last for more than an hour and a half, schedule in a five-minute coffee stop so everyone can refresh themselves (including the minute-taker!). This also helps structure the meeting and will usually speed it up, as the break on the agenda means everyone knows that a particular point has to be reached by coffee time.

The right environment

Although there's usually not much choice, wherever possible choose a room that will be comfortable. This will make the meeting easier to chair and to minute, and it is more likely to be productive. The room size and layout should be appropriate, and the room light and airy with minimum distractions. See Chapter 6 for more information.

Refreshments

Make sure that coffee and tea are available at the start of the meeting, and encourage the chairperson to make sure that everyone has some and then have the tray taken out. This should prevent the one-by-one drift back for refills, which is distracting for all. A short 'coffee stop' should be built into longer meetings (see above). Water should be available throughout.

Equipment

Make sure you know what equipment is required by participants (eg laptop, whiteboard or flipchart), so this can be booked. It is always a good idea to have a flipchart in a meeting room, as it can be used to list ideas or problems. Listing the latter is a good way of taking the heat out of an argument; focusing on the flipchart stops people focusing on one another and slows the pace.

Prepare a master checklist of absolutely everything you might need to do. For each meeting you arrange, print off a copy and, as you set up the meeting, cross out the things that are not relevant and then tick off the tasks as you do them.

Receiving apologies

Apologies can be received at three stages:

- When the future date is set at the end of the meeting, someone may say, 'I can't make it but you carry on.' This is not minuted or mentioned on the agenda for the next meeting (unless you choose to show a circulation list). However, it should be listed as an apology for the next meeting.
- At any time before the next meeting.
- Via someone else on the day.

You should also include those who know you are aware, for example, of their holiday, even if they do not specifically relate this to the meeting.

When committee members send apologies for a meeting, check whether they were responsible for any item on the agenda. If it is a general item, it can usually be dealt with in their absence but if their input is necessary, the item should be deferred to the next meeting.

It's also a good idea to check whether they had spotted any errors in the previous minutes or had any action points and find

out their progress. You or the chairperson can then report on their behalf at the meeting. You might also want to ask whether they have any comments on agenda items which should be given on their behalf, or even whether they wish to put an item on the agenda to be discussed in their absence.

SUMMARY POINTS

- Build administrative systems to enable efficient management of diaries, e-mail, etc. Time spent in setting these up is well-rewarded in time saved using them in future.
- Allocate and prioritize time to getting information from participants, for agenda creation and for general administration of the meeting.

3 Sections of a meeting

Meetings need to be structured if they are to be effective. That is not to say that the structure has to be overt, seeming to be more important than the content. Compare it to a day in the city with your family. It is likely to be more successful if you know what you want to visit and in what order, but you can present this as either, 'It's 3 o'clock, time to move on to the museum; we've been here for an hour', or, 'Let's go and have a look at the museum.' One sounds like the timetable ruling the day, the second like a good idea!

Formal meetings are likely to have a more obvious structure. For informal meetings the chairperson might not want to appear so dictatorial. However, it is having an underlying plan that will keep the meeting to time and productive; the skill is to avoid drawing attention to the structure.

Some of the sections of a meeting might sound out of date or too formal to you, and most can be changed to suit specific purposes and styles. The overall process is to:

- sort out the administration;
- confirm the past;
- deal with current issues;
- deal with last-minute issues;
- plan for the future.

The sections of the meeting are outlined below together with suggestions for how to make them seem more modern and/or less formal. You do not need to use every section for every meeting but at least you can make an informed choice and use the ones that are appropriate. However, whichever you use, they are usually kept in this order.

Welcome

The introduction is the point where the chairperson gets the meeting under control and started.

The chairperson should:

- call the meeting to order on time;
- give any 'housekeeping' information;
- explain the purpose of the meeting if it is a one-off;
- give any other 'introductory' information.

What to listen for

There is not usually anything to minute at this stage and so, although it should be done by the chairperson, it doesn't usually appear on the agenda or minutes.

Occasionally the welcome is used for a specific purpose worth minuting and if this is planned it should appear on the agenda.

Apologies

'Apologies' is the opportunity to clarify who is, and is not, at the meeting. The names of those who have said they will not attend are usually given by the chairperson or secretary, but others may be added by participants.

The chairperson should:

- ask participants to introduce themselves;
- clarify whether those who are not present have given apologies;
- ascertain whether there are representatives for those not attending;
- re-organize the agenda if a participant's absence means an item cannot be discussed;
- check whether the meeting is quorate, if appropriate (that the necessary number of people are present – as laid down in the terms of reference).

What to listen for

It is essential that you have a complete list of those who attended as well as those who did not attend (and whether they had sent apologies). Make sure you are aware of anyone who has sent a colleague in their place. To ensure your record is complete, have a list of those who should attend and make this your start-point, rather than just noting the names of those who are there and those who are named as apologies. See the section on 'Finding out who's who' in Chapter 6 for more guidance on how to do this.

Speak out!

It is essential that you get the names at the meeting (don't rely on others remembering who was there). It is entirely in order for the minute-taker to ask for introductions, but the easiest way is to pass around a signing-in sheet (see Chapter 6 'Attending the meeting' for guidance on this).

Committee business

This section is for business that relates to the committee rather than to its purpose in meeting. It is likely to involve changes to the:

- *structure*; for example:
 - discussion on how a committee should be made up;
 - changes to take into account a merger with another organization.
- *function*; for example:
 - changes to the remit of the group;
 - discussion as to whether the group still has a purpose;
 - confirmation that a part of the group's work is no longer necessary.
- *personnel*; for example:
 - resignations and new members joining;
 - long-term substitutions (to cover maternity or sabbatical periods);
 - confirmation of roles within the group.
- *administration*; for example:
 - a change of chairperson;
 - alteration of frequency of meetings from monthly to quarterly;
 - change of venue from always at head office to a rotation between divisional offices;
 - the possibility of doing without 'Any other business'.

This is a main business item and should always be minuted in the same style as the rest of the minutes. If there is more than one item you can list them as subheadings under the main heading of 'Committee business' or as sequential items with relevant headings.

It is best to give this section a relevant title (eg 'Administration', 'Resignation', 'Long-term future of [name] group').

Declarations of interest

There may be an item on the agenda to which a participant cannot contribute because of some conflicting interest. There should be a rule laid down for this (whether the individual should leave the meeting or just cannot contribute to the item) but, if it is a one-off situation, the group may need to decide the appropriate approach. The chairperson should:

- ask participants for any interests that need to be declared;
- either decide or ask for group decision on the action that should be taken.

What to listen for

You should note who declared an interest, what it was and what was done about it. The options are usually that the person either:

- resigns from the commitee;
- leaves the meeting for the relevant item (or the whole meeting);
- stays in the room but not speaking on the item (this is not an ideal approach because someone can communicate a great deal non-verbally and participants may be unhappy making a decision when the person who will be affected by it is watching);
- joins in all aspects of the discussion and decisions because the conflict is deemed to have no bearing.

It is important to be clear in the minutes whether the person 'abstained' (stayed in the room, non-contributing) or 'withdrew from the meeting' (left the room).

Many groups also maintain a register of interests which is updated regularly (often annually) and may be added to as potentially conflicting interests arise. This can be managed through the meetings or as a separate administrative task. It is important to be clear that this is separate to the check for potential conflicts relating

to current agenda items – it is one thing to maintain a list, another to apply its contents to the business of the day.

Minutes of previous meeting

This is where the minutes actually become 'Minutes' where the group take responsibility for them.

Although it can seem that this section is designed solely to humiliate the minute-taker, there are actually two very good reasons for having it. The first is to *confirm that the minutes are accurate*. Time should not be wasted with corrections to grammar and punctuation; it is the errors of fact that should be noted (eg showing £5,000 as £5,500 may be a typing mistake, but it has the appearance of fact and is worth minuting).

The second reason is to *prevent individuals changing the minutes without the knowledge of the group*. If you take pre-meeting corrections from individuals you may end up with conflicting changes. More importantly, people will be changing the minutes without the knowledge of the rest of the group and the final copy will not be the one that everyone has seen. The chairperson should draw attention to any changes already notified and individuals should add any other points. That way, changes can be debated and will be clearly shown in the minutes.

Minutes are seldom signed these days. If they are, it is done by the chairperson at the meeting. The purpose of signing is to demonstrate further that everyone at the meeting signalled their acceptance of the content – the chairperson signs on behalf of the other participants. If the minutes are not bound, they should be signed on the front cover and initialled on every other page.

Time is often wasted on this part of the meeting, either because participants start reading the minutes or because the chairperson guides them through, page by page. With this approach, people are looking for 'mistakes' so it is no surprise that they make changes.

They will also spot things to talk about and start unnecessary discussion, and may give feedback on actions and other things that have happened since the last meeting. People will also give updates on their actions, causing confusion between this and the next section. The chairperson should:

- ask at the end of a meeting for minutes to have been read before attending the next;
- ask the group whether they approve the minutes;
- get group agreement to any changes that are suggested;
- ask for final approval after all changes have been agreed.

What to listen for

Take a copy of the previous minutes into the meeting and just note the changes on it. These can then be typed up into the current minutes back in the office.

Speak out!

As this is the section where the minutes actually become *the minutes* it is essential that you are able to record their approval. If the chairperson doesn't actually ask the questions, you will have to interrupt; eg 'Excuse me, do I note that the minutes are now approved?'

The heading for this section seldom changes, but you can use headings like 'Confirmation of minutes' or 'Approval of minutes'; you can change 'previous' to 'last'; or you can include the date: 'Minutes of the meeting held on [date].'

Matters arising

'Matters arising' is one of the most misunderstood sections of the meeting. One of the key reasons for having minutes is to provide

an audit trail of what was done about the issues discussed and it is this section that meets this essential requirement. Increasingly, groups use a more relevant heading such as 'Update on actions'. Every action that is due for completion on or before the meeting date should be confirmed as having been done or, if not, what will be done to complete the task (and by when). If someone has encountered problems, these can be discussed and a new or amended action given if necessary. It may also be the case that something has changed and it is no longer feasible to undertake the action at all.

If some of the action points relate to items that are also on the agenda, the relevant 'Matters arising' can be incorporated in those items. Make sure it is clear on the agenda what is an action to be followed up and what is business for discussion at the meeting (see Figure 3.1).

There may be a general item in previous minutes on which the group needs an update. This can also be included in 'Matters arising'. As a general rule, if it was agreed at the previous meeting that the person would find out some information and update the group, this should be an action and the update given as a 'Matter arising'. If it is a full-scale presentation or report that is to be given, it may be better to include it in the next section and just noted, 'See item X' under 'Matters arising' to cross reference it in the minutes.

Occasionally a whole meeting is justifiably 'Matters arising'. This is usually in project-planning-type events where each member

> **6. Open day**
> 6.1 **Matters arising**
> (a) Delivery of furniture for Year 9 classes
> (b) Availability of sports centre
> 6.2 **Catering**
> 6.3 **Musical performances**

FIGURE 3.1 Example incorporating 'Matters arising' into agenda item

is responsible for a particular aspect of the project. In this situation there should not be a separate section, but each agenda item should start with the matters arising for that subject before moving on to discuss current concerns and finishing with confirmation of the participant's next action(s). If there is new business it is usually taken after the regular items, and for the next meeting is included in the above process for the relevant person.

The chairperson should:

- directly ask each person whether they have completed their action;
- discourage long explanations of *how* the action was done;
- follow up incomplete actions by defining next stage (with clear deadline);
- confirm that a previously planned action cannot be completed and must be abandoned.

What to listen for

It is essential that every action is clearly followed up in the minutes so you should be listening for whether this has been done either formally, eg 'Yes, everyone has been told', or informally, eg 'Yup, sorted'. If an action is incomplete, listen for the next stage, the deadline and whether it remains the responsibility of the same person.

Speak out!

It is essential that the minutes provide a clear audit trail of actions so if you are not clear about whether something has been done, you will have to ask. Use a question like, 'Excuse me, for the minutes, can you confirm whether the teams have been identified?' Or, 'Excuse me, I haven't got a note of whether the budget was approved.' (In other words, no one has said!) See Chapter 4 'Agenda' for help with supporting this through subheadings on the agenda.

If you don't like the formal title, try 'Update on action points' or similar.

It is essential to be clear about the difference between 'Minutes of the previous meeting' and 'Matters arising', because so many chairpersons merge the two in a review of the previous minutes, page by page. This is poor meetings practice because people read at different speeds and look for different information, so the meetings can become shambolic and take a disproportionate amount of time.

- Minutes of the previous meeting is about the document: is it correct?

- Matters arising is about the people: have they done what they said they would do?

If the chair does merge the two in the meeting, take a copy of the minutes with the actions highlighted. As you get updates, note what has been done and note the next step where actions are outstanding. You should be able to quickly check your highlighted sections to make sure each has been dealt with. Take a bright pen to note any corrections made. When you type the minutes, separate the corrections and the action updates into the correct sections. If the agenda presents the sections as a merged 'Minutes of the previous meeting and matters arising', use two subheadings to separate them.

For information

Information items are those that are not for discussion, just to hear (or 'receive'). It may be that every participant updates on recent work (eg at a team leaders' meeting); or that just a few members have to report (eg finance report, health and safety report); or it can be a one-off. This latter type is when a member wants to give information to the rest of the group (eg giving feedback from a conference).

If the information is the first part of an item, for example the conference report-back precedes discussion on implementing the best practice learnt, it should be a main agenda item that the individual will start.

For a meeting, the most common problem with reports is their being given out and read on the day. It is difficult to take in detail when reading in a group and time is wasted with an argument often following as individuals focus on one point they have noticed.

If the information is as a result of a previous action

As a general rule, if it was agreed at the previous meeting that the person would find out some information and update the group, this should be an action, the information should be circulated prior to the meeting and this confirmed as a 'matter arising'.

If it was decided at the previous meeting that a presentation of the information is needed, it should be an 'information' item and under 'Matters arising' just type, 'See item X.'

Alternative headings include 'Reports', 'Information only' or 'Information items'.

The chairperson should:

- only accept paper reports that have been circulated with the agenda;
- assume that the reports have been read and only ask the person giving it if there is anything they wish to add (not to read it out);
- discourage discussion.

What to listen for

For paper reports, it is only necessary to report that they were given or received. You can use phrases such as, 'The group were updated on...' Verbal reports are usually fast, and sometimes rambling.

A summary should be minuted but the information is best obtained from the person before the meeting and then double-checked as it is given.

Agenda items

Although there have been several sections before the group gets down to the main business of the day, they should not take long. The main agenda items are the topics that group members have asked to discuss at the meeting.

The chairperson should:

- manage the people;
- manage the content/agenda;
- manage the outcomes;
- manage the time;
- support the minute-taker.

What to listen for

There is plenty on listening and note-taking later in the book but in summary: minutes are a summary of what was discussed, not what was said. They should comprise an explanation of the issue, if appropriate; a summary of the reasons for the decision that was made; the decision and the action that is needed to move the issue forward. See Chapter 9 for more information on the amount of information that is appropriate for minutes.

Speak out!

It is entirely acceptable for the minute-taker to interrupt for anything that is needed for the minutes, eg failure to hear, to understand or to keep up. It is *essential* that the minute-taker interrupts if the action is not defined. This means getting a clearly defined

'next step' that tells exactly *what* is to be done, the name of the person responsible for doing it and a deadline date. Sometimes the person taking the action isn't paying attention and will need minutes to tell them what it was they agreed to do so it will be a problem if the minute-taker hasn't got the information. See Chapter 11 for more information on actions.

Any other business

This section allows for last-minute items to be discussed. 'Last minute' means things that happened after the agenda was dispatched that cannot wait for the next meeting. It is not for items that a participant could not be bothered to submit. Sometimes an item may be held for 'Any other business' because the person raising it wants to discuss it without the others being prepared. This should be prevented by the chairperson – if the group members are not in a position to discuss something knowledgeably, that item should be deferred to the next meeting.

The chairperson should:

- start the meeting by asking for 'any amendments or additions to the agenda';
- place those items in an appropriate place within the agenda or in 'Any other business';
- reject any items that are not appropriate for discussion by the group;
- reject any items for which the group have not had the necessary preparation (eg not seen a report);
- reject any items that can wait until the next meeting.

It is worth considering whether 'Any other business' is needed. If it is used because people do not bother to follow items on the agenda, or keep them quiet in order to raise them suddenly at the

end of the meeting, it is best to remove it from the agenda. If last-minute items genuinely occur then it is a valuable section. If you do remove it, don't number 'Date of next meeting' on the agenda, so anything extra that is raised can just be added to the end of the minutes.

What to listen for

Keep a focus on the items that are relevant and ignore any other discussion. Note any items that are 'deferred to next meeting' and add them to the agenda.

Very occasionally, this section is called 'Late items' or 'Last-minute items'.

Date of next meeting

The chairperson should:

- arrange several months' meetings at a time;
- confirm the date of next meeting and remind them of deadline for agenda items;
- know the essential participants if a meeting has to be set up so a date they can manage can take priority.

SUMMARY POINTS

Make sure you are aware of the purpose of each section so that you can:

- take appropriate notes;
- ask for information that is necessary to minute for each;
- allocate information to its correct place in minutes if the meeting is not well structured.

4 Agenda

There are several reasons for having an agenda:

- To enable participants to prepare for the meeting.
- To ensure that everything important is dealt with.
- To guide through subjects in a logical order.
- To remind the chairperson of what to discuss.
- To make chairing easier through everyone being aware of the structure, order and purpose of each item.
- To give structure to the minutes.

The agenda is like a shopping list – without a list you tend to buy things that catch your attention at the expense of the mundane but necessary items. It takes much longer because you browse and have to backtrack when you remember something. And then you have to call in another day for things you have forgotten. A meeting without an agenda is the same: participants discuss the topics that catch their attention but forget to discuss what they are there for. It takes longer because the order is irrelevant and things that were forgotten or not completed get added to the next agenda.

It isn't easy to fit preparing the agenda into a busy schedule and, as a result, it is often not ready till the morning of the meeting. This means the participants will not be prepared and the result will be ill-thought-out debate, argument and poor decisions.

It is vital to spend time putting together a useful agenda and you should ensure that it is well structured and reasonable for the time available. Your efforts will be rewarded by a shorter, more structured meeting. Taking the minutes becomes easier and the time involved in typing them up is much reduced. The agenda should be circulated a week before the meeting.

The deadline for agenda items should be confirmed in the previous minutes under 'Date of next meeting' and the chairperson encouraged to refuse items that are not received by that date. It is essential that any papers that need to be read before the meeting are received in time to be circulated with the agenda.

Who should prepare the agenda

Although the agenda is the responsibility of the chairperson the work often falls to the minute-taker. Although this means another task to be done, it is considerably easier to minute a meeting if you have been involved in the preparation.

A few days before the agenda is to be circulated, e-mail the participants to ask if there are any items they would like included. Ask the chairperson for items and look through the previous minutes for anything which should obviously be carried forward. Draft the agenda and get the approval of the chairperson before circulating it to the group. Anything that arises after this is done should be included in 'Any other business' in the meeting.

Who receives the agenda

The agenda should be sent to all participants and, as a general rule, to those who are attending for the one meeting (in part or in whole) and observers. This is a courtesy and is not essential if there are concerns about confidentiality.

Layout

The basic layout of the agenda does not vary greatly from one organization to another. It is essential that it includes the name of the group that is to meet, the date, time and place of the meeting, and the headings of the different agenda items. If the group is not a regular committee, give a list of those invited to attend – a circulation list (this is usually only done for a one-off meeting).

HEADING

The heading can be either the traditional paragraph style (see Figure 4.1), or the much more common centred style (see Figure 4.2).

Give a closing time so everyone knows how long the meeting should take and give enough information about the venue to enable the participants to find it. For some meetings this could extend to a postcode, but it's usually just the room and floor number.

Agenda for the IT User Group meeting to be held on 21 June 2017 from 10.30 to 12.00 in Meeting Room 6, Emmerson House.

FIGURE 4.1 Paragraph-style heading

IT User Group Meeting

21 June 2017, 10.30–12.00
Meeting Room 6, Emmerson House

AGENDA

FIGURE 4.2 Centred heading

What to include on the agenda

The basic agenda is by far the most common style in use today; sadly it is also the least effective. The headings tend to be quite vague and as a result participants could discuss their interests or concerns under more than one heading, so subjects will almost inevitably get discussed twice (or more). These general headings mean that people will have different ideas of what needs to be covered, so the discussion is likely to be muddled and some aspects may be left out altogether. An example of the basic agenda is given in Figure 4.3.

Facilities and Administration Committee

29 May 2017, 3.30–5.00 pm, Meeting Room 3

Agenda

Apologies

1. Administration

2. Minutes of the previous meeting

3. Matters arising

4. For information

5. Visit of David Smith MP

6. Car parking

7. Canteen

8. Post delivery

9. Any other business

10. Date of next meeting

FIGURE 4.3 Basic agenda

Full agenda

A full agenda gives more detailed information, specifically as detailed in the following sections.

SUBHEADINGS

- *For matters arising*
 As the minute-taker, you are responsible for recording whether actions agreed at the previous meeting have been completed. This is a vitally important part of your role to support the minutes in their purpose as an audit trail. It can however be difficult to achieve as the group tend to work from the previous minutes. The different speeds of reading, people's tendency to look ahead for the items which interest them and the hope of some to avoid admitting they've forgotten to act mean that the feedback is all over the place. On the agenda, list the actions that are due for completion, together with the name of the responsible person. This will enable the chairperson to work through the list and you can easily pick up on any that are missed. There is the bonus that people get an extra reminder that they had an action so may be able to get it done in time. An example of this is given in Figure 4.4.

```
3.  Matters arising
    3.1  Canteen tables        D Simmonds
    3.2  Menu boards           M Daniels
    3.3  Car park lighting      T Young
```

FIGURE 4.4 'Matters arising' with subheadings

- *For reports*

 Simply number and list the topics for reports and the name or initials of the person reporting.

NOTES OF PAPERS THAT ARE ATTACHED

Any papers that are to be read before the meeting must be sent out with the agenda and should be listed by the relevant agenda items. This column can be headed 'Papers', 'Reports' or 'Attached'.

INSTRUCTIONS/GUIDANCE

If participants are required to undertake any action or consultation before the meeting, this can also be listed by the relevant item. This can be in the same column as the papers, in which case the heading is usually 'Notes' (papers are then listed as 'Paper attached').

LEAD SPEAKERS

Many items will start with specific input from a participant, either a formal report or an informal update or explanation. Where this is the case, show the name on the agenda. This gives the chairperson guidance on who to turn to, and prevents participants making too early a contribution (possibly having misunderstood the subject).

Where the item is for general discussion, do not put a name, even if one person highlighted the need to discuss it. If that person has nothing specific to say, time will be wasted if he or she rambles on.

Names must be placed alongside items in Matters Arising and information items (showing who was responsible for the action and who is to report).

OBJECTIVES FOR AGENDA ITEMS

One of the most useful things to include on the agenda is an objective for each item. This changes the focus from *what* is to be discussed

to *why* it is to be discussed. Some agenda items will have just one objective, but if there are various aspects of an item to be dealt with, there may well be more. Although this creates more work before the meeting (finding out the purpose of items as they are given for the agenda), the improved focus of the meeting and increased ease of minute taking makes it well worthwhile. Figure 4.5 shows an example of an objectives agenda.

USEFUL WORDS

There are some phrases that come in useful for an objectives agenda, and you will no doubt find more. Choose the word that is most appropriate for the type of discussion or desired outcome necessary:

	where the group are to:
to receive	be told (eg a report)
to decide*	decide the outcome at this meeting
to agree*	agree the outcome at this meeting (ie the same as decide)
to confirm	confirm an earlier choice or the choice of another group
to approve	approve an earlier choice or the choice of another group (ie the same as confirm)
to discuss	talk about
to select*	choose between alternatives
to establish	find out
to resolve*	sort out (usually a problem)
to explore	talk about (ie the same as discuss)

*Items that use these words are required to result in an action point.However, any other objective may result in an action point if that proves the appropriate outcome.

With an objectives agenda you know where decisions are required, and it is considerably easier to listen for them and, if necessary,

Facilities and Administration Group

29 May 2017, 3.30–5.00 pm, Meeting Room 3

Agenda

Apologies

1. **Administration**

 To review arrangements for minute taking

2. **Minutes of the previous meeting**

3. **Matters arising**

 3.1 Canteen tables D Simmonds

 3.2 Menu boards M Daniels

 3.3 Car park lighting T Young

4. **For information**

 4.1 Health and safety annual review (attached) R Budgeon

 4.2 Staff forum D Simmonds

 4.3 Administrative management course R Davies

5. **Visit of David Smith MP**

 5.1 To confirm timetable for visit (attached) R Davis

 5.2 To agree strategy for maximizing publicity R Budgeon

 5.3 To discuss security implications of visit T Young

6. **Outdoor smoking area**

 6.1 To decide future of outdoor smoking area

7. **Canteen**

 7.1 To draw up plans for redecoration

 7.2 To confirm style of chairs (attached) D Simmonds

 7.3 To discuss provision of (consult

 magazines colleagues)

8. **Post delivery**

 8.1 To consider problems following merger

 8.2 To agree standards for delivery frequency (consult

 colleagues)

9. **Any other business**

10. **Date of next meeting**

FIGURE 4.5 Example objectives agenda

remind the chairperson of the necessity to decide. Remember that it is an essential part of your role to get the actions that are agreed, so if you are not clear you will have to ask. It is easier to do this if the agenda shows where actions are expected; just ask 'Is there an action that you'd like me to record?' or 'I have nothing for the decision on item X' – a polite way of pointing out they haven't defined it, or maybe have forgotten it altogether.

A logical order for agenda items

A group that jumps from one agenda item to another and back again causes great problems for the minute-taker, but sometimes the fault lies in a poorly designed agenda.

There is no 'right' order, but it is generally preferable to deal with important items first. This is to help achieve useful discussion while everyone is fresh and focused and also in case time runs short at the end. The overriding order should be one of decisions needed. Where a decision on one item will have an impact on the discussion or decision of another, the agenda must be structured to allow for this.

Look out for items that are closely linked and should follow one another or those that are basically the same and can be incorporated as one item, perhaps with subheadings.

If some people will have to do a lot of talking, it may help to split their agenda items to give them a rest and to give others a change of voice to listen to.

Timing the agenda

Timing the agenda provides a reminder for the chairperson and empowers the group to self-manage if the chairing is weak. If an item is running over time, it may seem rude for someone to point this out – as though they were simply bored. Having the timings on the agenda make it easier for someone to draw attention to the clock. The times also send a general message of time being important.

Some groups find that including times for items on the agenda is worthwhile. If you do this, use real time (10.15, 10.35) rather than time allowed (20 minutes, 15 minutes), so that it is easy to judge whether the meeting is on time. (See Table 4.6.)

Timing the agenda means that everyone can see how much time is allowed and gives an indication of the relative importance of each item. It also enables the chairperson to use the excuse of 'not much time' to quieten a dominant group member in a less personal or aggressive way than asking that member to be quiet.

Ask those with agenda items how long they need for the discussion (without giving any guarantee that they will have that time!). This means that you can assess the amount of time needed before the meeting starts and address any problem of shortage of time. This has the added advantage of reminding participants that time is important.

Timing the agenda serves little purpose when ignored by the chairperson and participants, so is only worth the effort if used.

Use descriptive headings and numbering

When you decide on headings for the agenda items, choose wording that will indicate to participants exactly what will be discussed. Far too many agenda headings are very general; for example 'Car parking'. This could be understood as being to discuss increasing the charges for parking, resurfacing the car park, re-designing the car park, replacing signs, creating a visitors' car park, decreasing the charges for parking, etc. Participants will come to the meeting with different expectations so the discussion will fracture before it's begun. For each item, ask the chairperson or whoever put it on the agenda for some more information and then make the heading more descriptive. For example, 'Car park charges', 'Resurfacing of car park', 'Signs for car park', etc.

The agenda items should be numbered with sub-numbering where appropriate (see the examples above). Keep a copy of the

Meeting	Facilities and Administration Group	Date Time	29 May 2017 3.30–5.00 pm
Place	Meeting Room 3		**Agenda**

		Apologies		
	1	**Administration** To review arrangements for minute taking		
	2	**Minutes of the previous meeting**		
	3	**Matters arising**		
	3.1	Canteen tables		D Simmonds
	3.2	Menu boards		M Daniels
	3.3	Car park lighting		T Young
3.45	4	**For information**		
	4.1	Health and safety annual review	Attached	R Budgeon
	4.2	Staff forum		D Simmonds
	4.3	Administrative management course		R Davies
3.55	5	**Visit of David Smith, MP**		
	5.1	To confirm timetable for visit	Attached	R Davies
	5.2	To agree strategy for maximizing publicity		R Budgeon
	5.3	To discuss security implications of visit		T Young
4.15	6	**Outdoor smoking area**		
	6.1	To decide future of outdoor smoking area		
4.25	7	**Canteen**		
	7.1	To draw up plans for redecoration		
	7.2	To confirm style of chairs	Brochure	D Simmonds
	7.3	To discuss provision of magazines		
4.40	8	**Post delivery**		
	8.1	To consider problems following merger		
	8.2	To agree standards for delivery frequency		
4.50	9	**Any other urgent business**		
	10	**Date of next meeting** *Please bring availability for w/c 29/7/17*		

FIGURE 4.6 Table layout for agenda

agenda in front of you throughout the meeting so that you can reference in your notes any item taken out of place or duplicated, by its number.

If you plan to present 'Apologies' at the top of the minutes, alongside 'Present', make sure it is not numbered on the agenda or everything will be out of order by one number.

Layout and presentation

The agenda is the advertisement for your meeting. If it looks scruffy and unprofessional, you will discourage those who are to attend. It should be presented so that the page does not look overcrowded, with headings sized in relation to their relative importance, appropriate widths for columns and so on. The examples above give an indication as to the generally preferred layout.

A circulation list

If the same group attend each meeting, there is no point in showing a circulation list. If someone is to attend for a specific item, this can be shown on the agenda (see Figure 4.7). If the meeting is a one-off event, or if there are several visitors, it is worth indicating who will be attending.

If the agenda is being circulated to external visitors, it may be worth showing who attends for their benefit. If you prefer, this can be done as a separate note.

Chairperson's brief

This is just a more detailed agenda, drawn up to help the chairperson manage the meeting. It will highlight exactly what is required from each section, how long to allow for it and any other information that will help, including background briefing notes if necessary.

8. **Post delivery**
 Irene Maddox, Post Room Manager, will attend
 8.1 To consider problems following merger
 8.2 To agree standards for
 delivery frequency consult colleagues

FIGURE 4.7 Example showing visitor to meeting

The brief is hardly ever used today, apart from for the most formal of meetings, but it could help a less experienced chairperson or one who has little time to prepare.

The minute-taker and chairperson should get together for a few minutes to discuss the meeting, flag any potential problems and agree how the meeting will run. Although this is seldom a formal meeting, it is a valuable aid to minute taking and helps remind the chairperson of the importance of your role.

It is generally best to have a detailed agenda for everyone's use. It helps the chairperson, empowers the group to self-direct if necessary and gives a tool to the minute-taker to support interruptions where clearly needed information is not given.

A short-notice meeting (or when there is no agenda)

It is entirely legitimate for the minute-taker to ask at the start of the meeting for the items (or aspects of the issue) that will be discussed. Although this doesn't create an agenda, it does give some structure for what will follow. If the chair does nothing to say what will be covered, use a question such as, 'To help me with the minutes, could you give me an overview of what you will be talking about today.' Or, 'Please can I have a list of the topics you are going to cover today.'

SUMMARY POINTS

- A basic agenda is only marginally more use than no agenda.
- Every heading should be descriptive.
- It should be clear where the chairperson needs to turn to a specific participant to introduce or explain an item.
- Participants should be able to see the relationship between the papers they have and the items they will discuss.
- Objectives for agenda items are an invaluable support for the chair, minute-taker and participants.

5 Personal preparation

It is difficult to find time to prepare for a meeting; it is often a case of finishing the phone call and dashing in. Of course you may not even know that you are to minute the meeting until just beforehand. Plenty of people think 'anyone' or 'any administrator or secretary' can take the minutes and you might find yourself called in with no notice. Despite the difficulties, time spent on preparation is usually recouped at the meeting and afterwards when typing the minutes.

Read the agenda

Rather than just skimming over the subjects, read through each item and consider what will be discussed, what terminology will be used and so on. If you identify any problem areas, ring or meet to get background information or any other help you need. Just raising awareness of your concerns may encourage others to be sensitive to your difficulties.

Read the papers

Ideally, you should be able to find the time to read papers in depth so you are familiar with the language and the content. In reality,

it is more likely that you will only have time to scan them. At least do this, as you will then know what type of information is there and may pick up details to help you at the meeting. It is a good idea to encourage the use of a cover sheet for papers. You can request whatever administrative information you need but, most importantly, should include a summary of the report. This can then be copied into the minutes, leaving you free to just listen in the meeting without having to take notes.

Talk to the chairperson

Meet with the chairperson, either formally or informally, to discuss what is to be covered, where decisions are expected, what style of minutes is required and how you are required to behave (eg can you interrupt?). This is also your opportunity to ask for any specific help or general guidance you may need. Don't fall into the minute-taking trap of being purely reactive. A proactive approach to your communication with all participants will not only yield greater understanding, it will earn you respect as a useful, involved and interested part of the group.

Talk to the contributors

It is not enough to understand the words on the agenda; you have to know the context. For example, you might understand the words 'Holiday cover for support staff' but you need to know which holiday. Who do people think should provide the cover? What's the budget likely to be? How many are needed? And so on. It may be that the person who has raised the subject has no idea, and that is why it is on the agenda, but often people do have some thoughts and it is useful to be aware of them.

Rather than ask specific questions and find you have misunderstood the words, start with something general (you could ask: could

you give me some background? Why is it an issue? Are you looking for a decision at the meeting?). You can always follow up with specific questions if you need to. You will also often pick up useful abbreviations or acronyms at this stage which will help in the meeting.

Talk to others

If there is an 'expert' who can help you with information on any agenda item you particularly fear, take the trouble to ask for help.

Consider who's who

In terms of knowing who you will be working with, meeting participants are likely to fall into three groups:

1 Those you know well (you'd recognize them out of context; for example in the supermarket). You don't need to give any further thought to these.

2 Those you've met, but would struggle to recognize out of context. Before the meeting, remind yourself of what they look like, consciously putting name to face in your mind. This will enable you to recognize them as soon as you see them and you will find it easier to remember their names when taking the minutes.

3 Those you haven't met. Try to find out what they look like by asking colleagues. Even if you cannot get any information, you have narrowed these to a smaller, more manageable group, and can approach them and introduce yourself promptly on the day. If you find it difficult to talk to strangers, plan a couple of open questions (those that start with what, where, when, how or who) to get the person chatting.

Confirm the administrative arrangements

If the arrival of coffee or booking of equipment is a problem in your organization, double-check the arrangements – much less stressful than wondering if something will arrive as planned.

Remind reception of visitors to your meeting

You should meet visitors who are attending the whole meeting – a good chance to establish personal contact. Those who are coming in for one item only can be directed as you wish.

Get the equipment together

Make sure that you have enough paper, suitable pens or pencils, a clipboard if there is no table, the attendance list and your copy of the agenda and papers. You might also want a copy of the last minutes (or even earlier ones) and spare agenda and minutes for those who have forgotten theirs. It is also worth taking the phone numbers of anyone you might have to call: to tell them that it's time to come in, to locate the coffee, etc.

Signed minutes

If the minutes are to be signed, take a copy to the meeting. This is the 'file' copy, not yours or the chairperson's. Take a working copy of the minutes for your own use for reference and so that you can note corrections and type them up later. If you are not using an action log, and the agenda doesn't list actions, mark them up clearly in your copy of the minutes so you can quickly find them when needed.

Last-minute minute-taker

Personal preparation is certainly recommended, but is not possible if you are called in at the last minute. Assuming you cannot refuse, say that you are happy to help and immediately ask for the help you will need. This is usually one or all of the following, but you can ask for more if you want:

- sight of the agenda and a verbal explanation of the headings;
- guidance on the depth and style of minutes required;
- introduction to the participants;
- ongoing summarizing.

It is quite acceptable to point out that you do not have a full knowledge of the subject but make your voice tone warm and strong so that it does not sound as though you are incompetent or whinging.

Personal preparation checklist

To save yourself time, prepare a checklist that can be printed off and used for all meetings. You can use the checklist in Figure 5.1 or prepare one that meets your needs.

Meeting checklist

- ☐ I have read and thought through the agenda
- ☐ I have read/skimmed the papers
- ☐ I have spoken to contributors to understand the context of items
- ☐ I know where decisions are expected
- ☐ I've discussed the meeting with the chairperson
- ☐ I know what style of minutes I'm writing
- ☐ I've booked tea/coffee/lunch

 I've arranged:
 - ☐ flipchart (and paper/pens) or whiteboard
 - ☐ equipment for presentations
 - ☐ extension leads
- ☐ Reception knows who's expected
- ☐ I know the names of those I haven't met
- ☐ I've thought of a couple of subjects for conversations with 'strangers'
- ☐ I've double-checked the administrative arrangements

 I've got:
 - ☐ paper
 - ☐ pens/pencils
 - ☐ clipboard
 - ☐ the agenda
 - ☐ copies of the papers
 - ☐ minutes for my reference
 - ☐ minutes for signing
 - ☐ spare copies of minutes
 - ☐ spare copies of the agenda

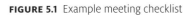

FIGURE 5.1 Example meeting checklist

SUMMARY POINTS

Before the meeting:

- Read the agenda properly.
- Read (or scan) the accompanying papers.
- Contact individuals to find out the background to their items and their expectations of the meeting.
- Be proactive in liaising with the chairperson.
- Read the previous minutes.
- Ensure the administration is complete (coffee bookings, etc).

6 Attending the meeting

Most minute-takers do not like the task. Many hate it. Quite apart from the difficulties of taking notes, they are uncomfortable within the group, often feeling out of place.

If, as minute-taker, you are respected by the group and treated well by them, this chapter is not for you. For a great many people, attending the meeting as a mute or non-contributing minute-taker can be daunting, particularly when working with a new group or one where the participants are very senior.

You would be unlucky to suffer from all the problems that follow, but most people have encountered one or two. Most of them stem from a less-than-competent chairperson, one who lets the meeting leave the agenda, allows the loud to dominate and fails to draw in the quiet. Most difficult of all for the minute-taker is the chairperson who does not take control and does not summarize the discussion (in fact this can cause problems for all the participants).

Where to sit

Some groups ostracize the minute-taker, even to the point of making him or her sit at a separate table. On other occasions it is the minute-taker who would rather be invisible and hides in the

corner. As minute-taker, you are part of the 'management team' for the meeting and your place is next to the chairperson.

Claim your seat

Make sure that you get to the room early to reserve your seat. If you work for an organization where everyone wants to sit by the chairperson, leave something personal in your place – an old purse with a bit of change in it or some car keys. People will move papers, a briefcase and even a handbag, but only the seriously determined will pick up someone's purse or wallet.

Finding out who's who

It is your responsibility to produce an accurate note of who attends the meeting and this can be difficult if you do not know everyone who attends. Although you are unlikely to have to put names or initials in minutes, it will probably help your recall of the meeting to have names in your notes. If you don't know who someone is, there are a number of things to try:

- *Use an attendance sheet*
 To avoid people signing illegibly, use a typed 'blank table' rather than a sheet of A4. Divide it into columns for the information you need, typically name (a column each for title, first name and surname) and department or organization. You may also want an e-mail address or phone number. If they still sign their names, add a first column for signature – most people will print after signing. You may find it helps to wait until everyone is seated and then pass the sheet around – you then get the names in order and can refer to someone by his or her seating position in your notes and work out the name later. For a larger meeting print the sheet on bright paper to prevent its getting stuck as it moves around the table. People will notice it!

- *Use name cards or labels*
 If you put out A5 cards, folded in half lengthways, and a few flipchart pens, most people will write their names without thinking about it. If this is not feasible, type a sheet of sticky labels with the names large enough to be read at a distance (unlike most identification badges). These can be given out on arrival or passed around. It is generally not advisable to plan the seating positions by placing name cards. People usually sit with their colleagues but don't think to move the cards. If this is the case for your meetings and you want pre-printed cards, just keep them by the door to collect on arrival.

- *Ask someone*
 It is always better to ask at the meeting because other people may not remember what someone looked like or what he or she was wearing.

- *Listen for clues*
 People will often give clues, saying things like 'How's life in Birmingham?' If you have prepared by reading through your list of likely attendees, you may well be able to work out who is who in this way. Even more obvious, listen for strangers being called by their name and you should be able to work out who each is.

- *Ask the stranger*
 It is not easy to approach people to find out who they are – it feels somewhat rude. However, it is a useful thing to do because it gives you a chance to familiarize yourself with their speech pattern. It also gives you the chance to present yourself as a confident professional. For your own comfort, don't leave anything to chance. Just saying 'Hello' does not exactly start a conversation. Trying to probe with questions like 'What's happening in your office?' may not bring the information you need. Introducing yourself is often met with a simple 'Hello', which again does not help. It is up to you to control the situation, and the best way is to introduce yourself and then ask directly

for the name: 'Hello, I'm Sally, the minute-taker today. Please could I have your name?' Have a pad to take a note of the name and then stay to chat for a few minutes or, if the person obviously does not want this, you can just thank him or her and move on. You are there in an administrative role and people expect you to administrate!

Whatever approach you favour, prepare by reading through the list of names to familiarize yourself and to identify potential problems such as hearing whether it's Lorraine or Elaine (people tend to say their names very quickly). Also look out for duplicated initials or names like Elizabeth/Liz where you need to decide whether to use E or L.

Remembering the name

Never tell yourself that you are dreadful with names – you'll come to believe your own negative publicity. Names are a problem because we seldom tie the name and the face together. We talk about people by name when they are not there, and we look at them in conversation but without using their name. We don't tie the two together. Try two simple techniques to help yourself:

1 Having asked for the name, use it once or at most twice in conversation or in thanking the person:
 - 'How long have you worked there, *Mr Hardacre?*'
 - 'Have you been to these meetings before, *Barbara?*'
 - 'Thank you, *Mrs Ratcliffe.*'
 - Don't use the name more than twice or you will sound insincere.

2 When you are not taking notes, either before the meeting or, for example, whilst people are arguing, look at each individual in turn and remind yourself of his or her name. Work round from one side of the table and, every time you get stuck, check with

your attendance sheet and go back to start at the beginning. The important thing is to combine looking at the person whilst saying his or her name (in your head, of course).

For all of these, it will help if you have studied the list of likely attendees and familiarized yourself with their names. It is easy to mishear a name if you are not prepared, and you will need to be alert for those who are substituting. If you hear or are given a name you do not recognize, you can then immediately ask whether that person is taking someone's place.

Not understanding

Above all, remember that you cannot be expected to know everything they know – if you did, you could have the meeting all on your own. It is perfectly acceptable for the minute-taker to not understand something! What is not acceptable is for the minute-taker to fail to take action to deal with it.

It is very uncomfortable to sit in a meeting with the subject matter going 'over your head'. In fact, it is not just the minute-taker who suffers from this. The various experts in the room may not understand one another, but no one likes to admit it. This can lead to some strange discussion and often to argument. As your experience with a group develops, understanding becomes less of a problem, but meanwhile there are some things you can do.

Before the meeting

If you spot something that worries you on the agenda, contact the person who wants to discuss it and ask for help. You might want to meet to discuss it, get hold of some background reading or ask for help afterwards – whatever suits you. You will also raise awareness of the potential problem and, it is hoped, the person will make things extra clear for you.

During the meeting

You should interrupt and ask for clarification. Useful questions include, 'Please could you:

- clarify... ?'
- explain... ?'
- put that in layperson's terms?'
- summarize... ?'

If possible, talk to people at the meeting, rather than wait a few days before ringing them. It's best to sort out problems while memories are fresh.

If interrupting is not appropriate, always make a note of what you don't understand. For example, 'He's talking about the IT problem that caused the crash last week', or, 'She's explaining the process for the capital planning meetings.'

After the meeting

If your problem is with facts, it is quite acceptable to talk to the relevant individual. However, beware of asking someone approachable for help in understanding an argument or discussion – you will get that person's view and run the risk of bias in the minutes. You should only approach the chairperson in cases like this.

Hearing

Reduce or remove any external noise by shutting windows or closing doors. Make sure that you can see everyone to establish eye contact where necessary and, again, sit by the chairperson because discussion usually slants that way. Try to arrange the table to avoid encouraging subgroups forming. For example, a long boardroom table will often encourage those at the end to start a different

conversation, as will a table that is too wide/square, when those on the corners will chat.

Minuting an argument

Many minute-takers panic and scribble furiously as argument breaks out. These notes are then discarded because the personal views and often inappropriate tone of the discussion do not appear in the minutes.

When discussion degenerates into argument, make a careful note of what is being 'discussed' and, if you want, add some extra information that you think will be useful; then stop and rest until order is returned.

Figure 6.1 illustrates the notes taken by a minute-taker during a 20-minute argument on whether to merge two departments. The minute-taker resumed taking full notes when the chairperson brought the meeting under control.

> *Merge admin and facilities?*
> - *not space to sit as one department*
> - *traditional bad feeling between them*
> - *who will be responsible?*

FIGURE 6.1 Example of notes taken during an argument

Skivvying

One of the most demeaning things to happen to a minute-taker is being sent out to photocopy or chase up the coffee. Quite apart from the negative message this sends, it is impossible to take notes

when not in the room. It is difficult to refuse without seeming rude, so the best approach is to pass the minutes to someone else. This should be done warmly but with a clear request, 'Please could you take notes while I'm out of the room?' The ideal person to pass to is the chairperson because he or she is the one who has the power to send someone else next time.

Coping with numbers/figures

Although it might be risky to say that you should not take notes of figures at all, this is a good general rule. Figures are hard to write accurately and even if you do have them correctly in your notes, you are likely to find a page of numbers and have no idea what they mean. Figures are like stories: they are given to make a point. Someone may give statistics over the past three years but the point is, for example, that the rise in redundancies is high/slight/tailing-off/increasing. It is better to understand, and note, the point – if you want the figures for the minutes, you can always ask for them later.

Maintaining concentration and focus

Few people mean to daydream; it is more common to 'come to' and realize that you have been thinking about something else. This usually happens when you do not understand fully or when the group are repeatedly going over the same points. Sometimes though, the cause is the opposite: getting too involved in the content and forgetting that you are there to take the notes.

Light and air

Make sure that the room is well lit and well ventilated. The latter may conflict with the need to close windows to cut out noise – consider the best balance for you in any particular room.

Temperature

Try not to let the room get too hot. If you think this is likely to be a problem, wear layers of clothes that you can shed with dignity.

Maximize understanding

It is much easier to concentrate when you understand what is being discussed, so make sure that you have read the previous minutes, the agenda and any relevant papers. If necessary, you can ask for guidance at the meeting if you feel out of your depth.

Refreshments

Keep to your normal levels of tea or coffee, but it is cold water that is most helpful in keeping you awake.

Remain part of the meeting

Sit forward, looking at those who are speaking so that you feel involved in what is going on.

Stay focused

Whether you lose focus because of daydreaming or getting involved, help yourself by sitting up with your pen ready to write. Although you must look up when a new person takes over the discussion, and eye contact is useful, generally keep your ears on the discussion, your brain on the meaning and your eyes on what you are writing. When you are not writing, look up but keep your hand ready. Avoid doodling.

Remember your stomach!

Don't eat a big meal before a meeting. Less obviously, avoid chocolate and other fatty sweets. Your body gets a 'chocolate boost' but

that is quickly followed by a slump as the sugar is cleaned out of your bloodstream. In addition heavy fats like this take a lot of your body's energy to digest, and most minute-takers would prefer that energy in their brain.

Use a break

If there is a short coffee break and you are getting tired, try to get moving – get the heart rate up a bit. Just walk swiftly up some stairs or along a corridor and back again.

The five things you MUST get in the meeting (asking later is too late)

1 **Who the people are**
 Never rely on asking the chairperson later; you will probably find they didn't notice who was wearing a particular tie, sitting in a specific place, etc.

2 **The approval of the previous minutes**
 If the chair goes through them and then moves on without actually stating that the minutes are approved, you must get the confirmation: 'Excuse me, do I record the minutes are approved.' That is the 'rubber stamp' of approval and it should come from the chair/group, not from your assumption. It must be done at the meeting because the chairperson's say-so later is not the same as the group agreement at the time.

3 **The follow-up of every action**
 People who've forgotten their actions are likely to keep quiet but the minutes are an audit trail and every action must be traceable from start to completion/abandonment. Don't confront the person, use a question like, 'Excuse me, I've nothing recorded for the action on 6.4?' Although it is the chairperson's responsibility,

you have to get the information for the minutes and asking tomorrow can be little help when it turns out that the person forgot to do their action – the rest of the group should have known about it.

4 The action itself

A clear definition of WHO is doing WHAT by WHEN. Again, it is probably not best to corner the person but ask, 'Excuse me, could you define the action for item 9?' or 'What is the deadline for giving the order?' Never rely on asking the person later – you might find they were daydreaming but didn't want to admit it and are now waiting for the minutes to tell them what they agreed to do. See Chapter 12 'Recording decisions and actions' for more information.

5 Explanations of vague terms

When someone says 'next year' do they mean calendar, financial or academic years? If they talk about 'here', do they mean in this building, this department, this sector, this town, county or region? These present a problem if you ring for more information the next day: you might find that everyone has a different definition!

Contributing minute-taker

It is difficult, if not impossible, to minute a meeting and contribute properly to it. Writing and talking are not activities that can be done at the same time. On the other hand, if you are a contributor to the meeting you are likely to have a higher level of knowledge of the subject. You also have the advantage of the status of group member, which makes it easier to interrupt and ask for help or information.

When taking notes you should not be writing down everything that is said by each individual. It is the topics discussed and the points raised that are of concern.

If you contribute to one item

Before the meeting, ask another member of the group to take minutes during your item. Try to remind the member of this before the item starts.

If you contribute throughout

It is simply not possible to take detailed notes and contribute. The group have to accept shorter (but no less accurate) minutes and an action point. You can reduce your notes accordingly. If this is not acceptable to the group, use 'Committee business' to schedule a discussion on how the meeting is run, present it as a problem and let everyone decide what should be done.

Since you have the status of contributor, if the chairperson does not summarize at the end of each item, you can interrupt and do so. Usually this is done by saying, 'Excuse me, can I confirm for the minutes… ?' You can even tape this, using a dictating machine, and you have the basis for your minutes. If the chairperson does summarize, this too can be taped (with agreement), but do not try to tape the whole meeting because it is extremely time-consuming to prepare the minutes.

SUMMARY POINTS

The minute-taker is not meant to have a view (unless contributing anyway), but that doesn't mean you must be silent. You must interrupt for the five key things and you should do so for *anything* you need for your notes – if you don't ask, they won't know you need help. Minute taking is a proactive, interactive, involved role, not that of a mute wallflower.

7 Working effectively with the chairperson and group

Many of the suggestions in the last three chapters are easier to implement if you have a good working relationship with the chairperson and members of the group. Minute-takers often complain that they are ignored by the people in the meeting, sometimes feeling like a second-class citizen, or even completely invisible. This is not usually the case; everyone has their own issues and concerns at the meeting and often they are simply thinking about themselves.

Everyone in a meeting is there because of the knowledge or experience they bring (or occasionally for the position they hold). The minute-taker is the same; you are there because of your knowledge and skill. You bring focus on what is needed for the minutes and knowledge of what is needed for them. Your skill is the note-taking: recognizing what to minute and, equally important, recognizing when you do not have what you need and asking. In the meeting situation, everyone should be treated equally with their salary and position in the hierarchy left outside the room. This applies equally to the minute-taker, but if you act as 'only the minute-taker' you will not earn the respect your role deserves.

Build a good relationship with the chairperson

Whilst the chairperson should take steps to liaise with and support the minute-taker, it is also the responsibility of the minute-taker to be proactive in communicating with the chairperson.

At all stages, maintain a style of verbal and non-verbal communication which sends a subtle message of 'we are in this together'. For example, asking, 'What deadline shall we have for the cut-off for agenda items?' (not, 'What deadline would you like me to give for...').

Be proactive in offering to help with the agenda (asking for items, drafting, etc) and find time to discuss the upcoming meeting as appropriate. This doesn't have to be a formal meeting; a brief conversation may well be enough to ask for what is needed or to bring the chairperson up to date with ongoing issues, apologies received, and so on.

Work to support the chairperson in the meeting by working calmly and effectively, making sure you present a professional image throughout. If you need to interrupt, do so confidently and clearly. Make sure you have all the papers and other documents you need.

After the meeting, type the minutes quickly and present any questions or problems as a collaborative discussion where you can. For example, 'I have a problem with item six; how should it be phrased?' (not, 'I missed loads in item 6. I didn't understand her. Can you help me put it right?').

What it's reasonable to expect from the chairperson

Most people who chair a meeting haven't thought through what they want from minutes or the minute-taker. Few mean to ignore you but most are so focussed on their own concerns and pressures

that they simply don't recognize the problems you are facing. It is reasonable to expect the chairperson to give you any help you need at each stage of the meeting, to support you and to lead by example in treating you with courtesy and respect.

Working with a weak chairperson

Most people receive no training in chairing a meeting; they usually take on the role through their work position or simply by looking up at the wrong moment. There is so much poor practice around that they cannot learn by example. On the surface, the role of the minute-taker is quite reactive, even silent; in reality, there is much you can do to guide the chairperson.

BEFORE THE MEETING

Be proactive in getting the agenda drafted and despatched. Look through previous minutes to pick up actions and ongoing issues to be included in the agenda. Show times, lead speakers and clear objectives to guide the chairperson (and to help the participants manage themselves).

Speak to the chairperson to ask for any specific help you need. If their chairing skills are weak, it is not worth overloading them with your demands so choose one priority need and ask for support in that area (eg summarizing, calming argument, introducing strangers). It is better to do this before a meeting because if you raise the issue after a meeting, it is difficult to avoid it sounding like criticism.

AT THE MEETING

The chairperson should manage each item so that it achieves its purpose. As the minute-taker's role is to demonstrate this, you can often achieve a lot through a well-timed, well-phrased question:

- The chair just asks for apologies but doesn't introduce people.
 - You can say, 'Excuse me, could I have everyone's names for the minutes?'
- The chair works through the minutes asking for corrections but forgets to ask for approval.
 - You can say, 'Excuse me, do I record the minutes are approved?'
- The chair forgets to check up on a couple of actions.
 - You can say, 'Excuse me, I've nothing minuted for the action for item seven.'
- After discussion, the group just drift onto the next item.
 - You can say, 'Excuse me, for the minutes could you clarify the decision for item eight?'
- The group decide something, but an action isn't allocated.
 - You can say, 'Excuse me, could you define the action for item nine?'
- The chair defines an action but doesn't say who is responsible or give a deadline.
 - You can say, 'Excuse me, for the minutes, who should I put as responsible for drafting that?' or 'What is the deadline for drafting it?'

AFTER THE MEETING

Type the minutes as soon as you can so the chairperson or group can help with any problems. Thank the chairperson for any help or support you were given and, if possible, comment favourably on things that went well.

Building a good relationship with the group

Work to ensure that you create the impression of calm, competence and confidence. Be warm and friendly to everyone in the group (even if it is not reciprocated) and call people by their name in greeting or if you have to interrupt.

Try to engender a sense of collaboration about the minutes (they are, after all, the responsibility of the group, not the minute-taker). For example, if your minutes are criticized or corrected with, 'You got my budget wrong on page 2', just reply with, 'No problem... what figure should I put?'

What it's reasonable to expect from the group

Like the chairperson, most are so focussed on their own concerns and pressures that they simply don't recognize the problems you are facing. It is reasonable to expect them to give you any help or information you request and to treat you with courtesy and personal respect.

Demonstrating confidence and competence

Get to the room first, ensure it is tidy and aired and make sure you are ready to greet people as they arrive. First impressions count so make sure yours is a good one on the day.

Dress

Wear clothes to blend in with the group. This is not necessarily your interview suit. If they wear pinstripes, a jacket is in order. If they're dressed in sweatshirts, you should dress down.

Of course it is important to be comfortable, to wear something that makes you feel good about yourself and wear 'layers' so you can shed with dignity if the room temperature rises!

Movement

Most people 'scuttle' when they are nervous, often hiding behind the papers they are carrying. Practise slowing your stride, straightening your back and lengthening your neck (think 'drop your shoulders' rather than pushing up from your hips).

How you sit

Sit by the chairperson and use your place at the table. Sit as though you are in control of your 'space'. Lean forward comfortably as you write and give yourself enough space for keeping your agenda and papers to hand.

Voice

Some people's voices rise with nerves, others go quiet and shaky; almost everyone gabbles. Very few think about how they sound until something has gone wrong and then they look back regretfully. Learn to speak clearly through a simple, three-stage approach:

Stage one

- In private, try speaking in a higher voice than usual, taking it as high as you can without squeaking, and then practise speaking lower than usual.
- Practise speaking louder than usual, without shouting, and then quieter.
- Try speaking faster than usual (think what you're going to say and then say it very fast), then try speaking slower.

- Spend two or three minutes doing this. You are working on getting your voice under your control. It doesn't matter if you feel foolish as long as no one is listening!

Stage two

- If your voice rises with nerves, when in a shop or a situation where you are not known, drop it just a little as you speak; if you tend to go quiet/shaky, speak just a little louder.
- Almost everyone should practise speaking slower. Say each word clearly and completely before saying the next; it may feel odd, but people understand you first time! Make sure you breathe in before you speak.

Stage three

- In your office or workplace, repeat stage two above. You shouldn't be so extreme that people notice; just moderate your normal speech a little.

By now you should have some confidence that you have control over your voice, so try the technique in more stressful situations. Before you know it you will be able to breathe/take control in any situation, and you'll find you have more presence and influence as a result.

Conversation

Greet people as you see them or as they arrive, using their names if possible. Before you attend the meeting, identify a couple of areas of small talk you can use to start a conversation. Open questions (starting with what, where, when, how and who) will help get people talking. If the group are talking before the meeting starts, go and join them. You don't have to contribute, but look at the speaker, smile and nod as appropriate. Remember who has a new job, new car or whatever as this will give you a personal conversation opener.

Eye contact

Look directly at people as you listen or talk to them. During the meeting, watch the speaker when you are not taking notes.

Expression

Make sure you do not frown in concentration or worry. Smile when you catch someone's eye, and develop a calm and interested expression that you can call upon when required (smile with your eyes, not just your mouth – practise in private!).

Coping with put-downs

Some put-downs are real; most are imagined. It is easy to assume someone has ignored you when in fact he or she was engrossed in thought and didn't see you. Always assume the best intention and best behaviour and react accordingly. Often this was the intention, and even if it wasn't, your dignity remains intact. A few examples are given below to illustrate this:

- Someone looks at you, and then pointedly at the tray, saying, 'Coffee?' The answer is, 'Yes, please.'
- You are sent out to copy something, make coffee or perform some task. Clearly hand the minutes to someone, asking him or her to take notes in your absence. The notes may not be much good, but you'll have made the point.
- Greet first, rather than waiting for someone to say hello to you. Use the person's name, and 'Hello' or 'Good morning' rather than 'Hi'.
- If you are passed by when papers are handed out, ask for a copy immediately. Try to prevent this in the first place by looking expectant and reaching out in anticipation of your copy.

- If you ask for help, for example an explanation, and get a response like, 'I suppose this is a bit beyond a secretary', smile sweetly and respond politely but firmly (eg 'I wasn't cut out to be an accountant'). You'll usually find the group sides with you and that there are a few smiles of support around the table.

No one puts you down without your permission, so when you are on the receiving end of an unpleasant comment just remember that they deserve your pity for needing to score a point on someone lower down the pecking order than themselves. No matter how you feel, NEVER put yourself down or apologize for existing.

SUMMARY POINTS

- Be proactive in your communication with the chairperson.
- Build relationships with the group members.
- Non-verbal and verbal impressions of you will have a significant impact on the way you are seen and treated so make sure you are sending good ones.

8 Taking notes

One of the greatest areas of concern for minute-takers is recognizing what should be noted and sifting out the irrelevant information.

Before you start to take notes, it is important to get the 'mechanics' correct. Handwriting, as such, is seldom taught in schools and as a result we fall prey to bad habits that leave us walking out of the meeting with a stiff arm, sore shoulder and often an unnecessary headache.

The mechanics of writing

- *Find a good pen or pencil*
 Ignore all the advice that pen is better, or pencil is what the experts use. You will write more quickly and legibly with the instrument that you like best. Experiment and then make sure you always take at least two into the meeting. Try to find one that has a rubber or ridged grip so that your hand does not slip, and that is not so narrow that your hand is pinched in holding it. Some people find it useful to take red or green pens to highlight actions or make other notes. If you can manage this and use the right colour at the right time, then it is worth trying. Otherwise, use symbols (eg an asterisk to highlight an action; a cross

or question mark in a circle to indicate a problem or question) or the layout of your notes to differentiate.

- *Sit properly*
 Sit back and 'square' in your chair so that your back and legs are supported.

- *Choose your paper*
 Most people would choose good quality paper so the pen glides over it without catching but others prefer a rougher recycled paper for the 'feedback' it gives as you write. Like the writing instrument, use whatever you prefer.

- *Support your arm below your elbow*
 Don't take your arm's weight on the wrist; after all, it's the joint that you need to move in order to write. Move in towards the table, so that the weight of your arm is taken just below your elbow. This frees your lower arm to move and will significantly reduce the arm and shoulder ache.

- *Use your non-writing hand to manage the paper*
 Don't leave the paper stationary and move your writing hand forward and back. Rather, keep your writing arm static (see the next section) and move the paper away from you as you work down the page.

- *If you don't have the 'luxury' of a table*
 Take a good quality clipboard so that the paper is well supported. Use a chair with arms and support your writing arm as above, moving the paper with the clipboard towards and away from you as you write.

How to take notes

Pen and paper

Pen and paper is still the preferred method for most minute-takers. It is simple, cheap and familiar.

ADVANTAGES

The main advantage is that you will have greater understanding and recall of the content because of the link between hearing and physically writing. The notes will be in your words and the symbols, abbreviations and acronyms are what you wrote as you heard their words.

Writing also encourages you to be mentally involved because you cannot possibly keep up with the speech so you are constantly evaluating what is said in order to write useful notes.

It is easy to move through your notes to return to an earlier topic to make additions if the group are jumping around the agenda, and if the paper is well used, there is no problem in adding extra points as they are made.

When you are typing the minutes, you can easily edit the notes, cross out items as they are typed and keep the notes and typing on the screen within sight.

DISADVANTAGES

It is not a particularly environmentally friendly means of note-taking. It can be difficult to keep up with the discussion if it is fast moving, although this is often a problem of writing the words, not the point. If your writing is not good you may struggle to read the notes back or you might find you've shortened words or sentences by only writing the first part which makes later understanding difficult.

Taking the notes

Decide on the type of pad you prefer: A4 or shorthand? Unbound, heat-bound or spiral-bound? Side bound or on the top? Wide or narrow lines (or plain, or squared)?

Rule the paper, about two-thirds or three-quarters of the way across to create a writing space that is about as wide as an A5 pad

with a separate 'junk' space on the right. This junk space can be used for arrows, asterisks, extra notes – anything that you don't want cluttering up your core note-taking space.

You might take it further and create a template with separate columns for noting discussions, decisions and actions. That works well with a good chairperson who summarizes, but more commonly you'll find that something you've noted in discussion becomes the decision and the system doesn't work out as planned.

If you think the group have gone off the agenda and are not sure whether to note the discussion, write it towards the right of the page. If it is needed then you have the notes but if it isn't you can quickly see what to delete.

If they return to an earlier subject, try to go back through your notes and add it where it belongs. You might find you have it already, they are just repeating a point, in which case there is no need to write anything.

Shorthand is NOT a help for minute-takers because you only build up speed when you stop thinking and just listen and write – just like fast typing, where you are not thinking of the keys you are hitting. Your minutes are not going to be a record of what was said and shorthand writers often end up with most of the words and little of the meaning. If you are lucky enough to work for a good chairperson who summarizes throughout and defines the decisions/action it can be useful because you simply listen to the discussion and take the summary as dictation. Most people who chair meetings fall far short of that gold standard!

Modern-day speedwriting is more help. It is not designed for dictation and will not enable you reach that level of speed. It is simply a means of writing what you would write anyway but around 30 per cent faster, using just the letters of the alphabet. It is learnt in a day and speed is built by incorporating it into your daily workload in a structured way.

Look for symbols that will save you time and build your use of these through practice. For example:

< > Less than, more than (or more/less)

+ add, plus, in addition, also, and, as well as

= equals, is the same as, same

≠ is not the same as, is different to

≈ nearly equal to, about the same as, roughly like

↑↓ rising/falling, top/bottom, up/down

∴ therefore

Abbreviate frequently used words, ideally to three letters. For example:

mtg meeting

agd agenda

mns minutes

dpt department

cte committee

chp chairperson

ppr paper

brd board

rpt report

Don't use first three letters; miss out vowels. It is easy to write 'com' and then not be able to remember whether you meant community, computer, commission, compare. Instd lv ot th vwls in lngr wrds if you cn rd thm bk. Always put the vowel in if it is the first or last letter of the word.

You may find it helps to write on the agenda, printing a copy with extra space if you want. If much of the meeting is related to the last one, take a copy of the minutes with a large margin and

> *Open at Christmas?*
> *Always closed between Christmas Eve and January 3.*
> *Everyone's closed, our customers and competitors.*
> *Complaints last year from customers who were working.*
> *We could pick up sales – but how many buy?*
>
> *It'll be quiet – always is – can catch up on paperwork.*
> *Several staff happy to work – We'll have to pay overtime*
> *– no, not necessary. It's working days, not bank hols.*
>
> *How could we decide who's working. The department*
> *could do it themselves. What if no one wants to work in a*
> *department? Not all need to be open. Which do? Sales and*
> *any others that want to.*
>
> *Many customers now are small businesses – we could pick*
> *up some orders as they'll be working. Stores need to be*
> *open – no point selling if can't deliver. So sales and stores*
> *to be asked to provide rota for staying open – skeleton*
> *staff. Others can work if want to.*

FIGURE 8.1 Don't write essay-style notes

add notes to that. If there are papers, you can make notes on them (but remember, you shouldn't normally be noting papers as they form part of the minutes anyway).

Use bullet points, not sentences.

If you write full sentences, you are likely to take down all the unnecessary 'filling in' words, often scribbling down the words that people say (see Figure 8.1). Not only will you have much that is not needed, but it will be harder to make sense of the notes, which will look like a school essay.

Write bullet points, working down the page, not across it (see Figure 8.2). If you write across the page, you are more likely to put in the 'padding' words and you will end up scribbling furiously as described above. Figure 8.3 shows an example of bullet points

Open @ Christmas?

Customers complained we closed. Pick up sales?
Not many. Catch up on paperwork? Staff happy 2 work
overtime? – no.

Who work? Departments to sort. What if don't want to?
Not all depts need to open... sales do and others who want
to. Might pick up some orders – our customers work.

Stores open – must deliver sales!

Sales and stores provide rota (skeleton staff) others
work if want to.

FIGURE 8.2 Don't write bullet points across the page

Open @ Christmas?
Customers complained we closed.
Pick up sales? Not many.
Catch up on paperwork?
Staff happy 2 work, overtime? – no.
Who work? Departments to sort.
What if don't want to? Not all depts need
to open…
Sales do.
+ others who want to.
Might pick up some orders –
our customers work.
Stores open – must deliver sales!
Sales and stores provide rota
(skeleton staff) others work if want to.

FIGURE 8.3 Work down the page, with plenty of white space for adding later notes

Open @ Christmas?
Customers complained we closed.
Pick up sales? Not many.
Catch up on paperwork?
Staff happy 2 work overtime? – no.
Who work? Depts to sort.
What if don't want to? Not all depts
need to open...
Sales do + stores
+ others who want to.
Might pick up some orders – our
customers work.
Sales and stores provide rota (skeleton
staff) others work if want to.

FIGURE 8.4 Organize your notes as you go

working down the page. Note the use of symbols and 'text speak' to aid speed.

As you take the notes, try to place them with related comments if you see them in time. If not, use arrows to link as you write. Figure 8.4 shows this with paper ruled for content.

Taking notes on a laptop

Increasingly minute-takers are using a laptop or even a tablet to take notes.

ADVANTAGES

The notes are already on the computer so there isn't the mental barrier of having to transfer them from paper. It is usually possible to type faster than write and it's easy to use the agenda as a template. If you can touch type, it is easy to maintain eye contact with the group which will aid hearing and understanding.

DISADVANTAGES

The risk of power or equipment failure, lack of familiarity with the keyboard, the difficulty of moving quickly though large amounts of text to return to earlier items to make additions or changes. Some people are fascinated by watching a typist at work and you may find yourself the subject of unwanted attention and you may be a distraction if you are a noisy typist.

Many people find the fact that they can type faster means they just take more notes but because typing does not really involve the brain, those notes do not remind so well of what was discussed... so more notes are needed.

PROJECTING THE MINUTES AS THEY ARE TYPED

Most minute-takers find this an appalling prospect but it can be useful if it is only decisions and actions that are to be taken. It makes the minutes a more collaborative exercise and can help if it is the chair or a member of the group who is taking the notes.

NOTE-TAKING

Make sure that you are near a power point and can safely keep the laptop plugged in.

Set the 'autosave' to one or two minutes and keep saving as you type. If you are worried about the machine freezing or failing, save to a new document at the end of each item so for a 12-item agenda, you will have 12 files, the first with only 1 item, the last with 12. If all is well, you can delete files 1–11; if there is a crash you are more likely to have kept the full meeting.

Use the agenda as a template for the minutes. Do as much preparation before the meeting as you can, entering the names and standard text. If you've been proactive and found out the issue for each item, get the introduction typed in before you start and, if an action is likely, create the layout ready to be filled in.

If you are likely to move back and forth around the agenda as the group return to earlier items, type a clear symbol or draw a line between items (tap underscore three/four times then 'return' and you should get a strong line across the page). These will be deleted earlier but will make it easier to spot a change of item as you scroll through the screen.

Concentrate on listening for the points (see later in this chapter) and avoiding the trap of using greater speed to get more unnecessary words.

Recording a meeting

This often seems as though it will be the answer to a note-taker's prayer – everything that was said, available at the touch of a button, but that is not necessarily the case. Some groups would not allow a recording, a few insist on it but a group must never be recorded without their knowledge and consent, and there may be an agreed approach to what will be done with the recording afterwards.

ADVANTAGES

Everything that was said is available and there is evidence if someone disputes the content of the minutes. If there are many figures, unfamiliar or technical terms it is comforting to be able to check them later.

DISADVANTAGES

It can be difficult to hear, particularly where people are softly spoken or talk over each other.

Some 'harder' voices come over much more clearly so their views may dominate the minutes in a way which does not represent the discussion. Similarly, sharp noises such as cups being put down or pens being clicked can mask the voices.

It is a very time-consuming (and boring) method of note-taking as you have a two-hour meeting to attend and then a two-hour recording to listen to. Going over sections repeatedly again takes time and it is easy to try to write up everything that was said, irrespective of its value.

If the group, or an individual, are uncomfortable with being recorded, doing so can influence the discussion and points may not be raised that would have been valuable to the discussion. Some will almost use sign-language to avoid being heard, or will get part way through a point and then back off as they remember the recording.

USING A RECORDER

Never record secretly, either using a recording system or your personal smartphone.

Never rely on the recording, there is a high risk of not being able to hear someone or the recording simply failing to record.

Ensure that you use the best possible equipment in terms of both recording and the microphone.

Place the recorder near you so that you can see the counter ticking up. At any stage where you feel you might need the recording, note the counter number and do the same at the start of each agenda item.

Smartpens

These link to a tablet or smartphone and incorporate a recording system. Using special paper with a dot pattern that tells the pen what you have written or drawn, your notes are synced to a tablet or to a computer as a PDF.

Once the notes are on the tablet, they can be turned into copy-able type which can be e-mailed for editing. At any stage, a recording can be made by touching a symbol on the special paper and will be played when that note is later 'tapped' on the tablet.

ADVANTAGES

The ability to turn on the recording as needed rather than having to search through a full recording will save time but the principle of getting permission to record remains.

Handwritten notes can be shared between all linked devices.

Although a little cumbersome to turn the notes to text, then e-mail them, then copy them into a document, it can be a time saver if your notes are legible to the system.

DISADVANTAGES

All the disadvantages of recording are the same with this system and there can be some noise from writing that can make it difficult to hear. The pen style and weighting may not suit everyone. Special paper is needed, although this can be printed providing a 600 dpi printer is available.

The biggest disadvantage is the difficulty in turning the notes into editable text in Word. There is a program to achieve this, MyScript, but it depends on legible handwriting and recognisable words and does not deal well with mathematical symbols. Since most notes in meetings are abbreviated, often scribbled, and involve symbols, the system is only useful for a few minute-takers.

Look as well as listen

Although you will usually be looking at what you are writing, it is important to remember eye contact:

- *Eye contact improves your hearing*
 It is easier to hear what someone is saying if you are watching as well as listening.

- *Eye contact reminds speakers of your presence*
 If you catch eye contact with speakers, they are reminded of your presence and are more likely to include you in their 'audience', which again makes it easier to hear.

- *Achieving eye contact*
 Although you need to look at what you are writing, when you hear the voice change, glance up and look properly at the new speaker, if possible catching his or her eye to demonstrate that you are listening. If you recognize that you have already noted a point, stop, look and listen, if necessary nodding encouragingly (a small movement!).

The message, not the words

It is essential to recognize that minutes are not a record of what is said; they are a record of what was discussed. They must be subject-based, NOT speech-based.

The key skill that a minute-taker needs is the ability to record the message, not the words. When someone is speaking, words come from the mouth, but the message comes from the brain. For example, the following people are all saying broadly the same thing (extracts from a discussion on the possibility of staying open over the Christmas holiday) – it is only the first one who ties up mouth and brain.

- 'Staying open between Christmas and New Year is worth considering seriously.'

- 'When I worked for Amercall, we always opened between Christmas and New Year and often picked up orders from competitors who were closed.'

- 'Quite a few staff are happy to work over the holiday period and take leave later in the year.'

- 'Several customers commented that they could not reach us during the Christmas fortnight.'

- 'Last year we lost several orders by not answering calls in the sales office over the holiday period.'

- 'Even if sales are quiet, it is one of the few times when we can catch up with the paperwork, re-organize systems and so on.'

- 'When I worked with the sales team, I used to hate the aftermath of the Christmas holiday. January low spirits combined with a rush of business, and the office was in chaos from a long shutdown after a chaotic Christmas party season. We always started the year with a backlog.'

As you listen to people talk, imagine saying to them '... and your point is?' That is what you have to work out when you are listening: what would they answer? Of course, you may have to actually ask this if you haven't understood but it will need to be done in a considerably more professional way!

As you listen, imagine you are holding a balloon with the current subject written on it – you are focusing on what they are discussing. Look back over the different comments made on whether to stay open over Christmas. They would have been prefaced by the chair saying something like, 'Item 12, Christmas Closure... now a few people have suggested we don't have the long closure this year; what do you think?' Your balloon would say, 'Open at Xmas?' and as everyone comments you can evaluate what they say and recognize that they are staying on that point but there's no outcome. Once there is an outcome you can note 'Yes, sales/ stores + anyone else who wants to' (and let go of that balloon). The chair might then ask, 'How are we going to staff it?' Now your balloon says 'How to staff?' and you might note some alternatives (imposed rota, staff to sort rota, lottery), but you are really waiting to find out the answer, which, finally revealed, is to ask the staff to sort it (and that balloon can go). The idea of the balloon is to help you keep focus on what you are listening for, rather than just scribbling the words people say.

Beware voice tone/delivery

Another aspect of listening for the message, not the words, is to take note of voice tone and delivery but not to be swept along by

them. For example, try saying the following sentence in a variety of tones, staged from neutral through to furious (you might want to add a few extra words): 'Most of the team don't know how to work the receiver.'

No matter how the words are said, the message remains the same. The minutes will have to be written in a neutral style so try to take the minutes in the same way; focus on the point being made, not the manner of making it. Have a look at the example quotes in the box, together with how they appeared informally in the minute-taker's notes.

'All the furniture in this office is old; it's scruffy and much of it is falling apart. We should do something about replacing it. It looks dreadful and one day there's going to be an accident.'

The office furniture needs replacing

'The phones must be answered by a human between 9.00 and 5.30; voicemail is only acceptable outside working hours. People don't like leaving a message and it gives the impression that we're keeping them at arm's length.'

Voicemail outside office hours only

'The goldfish have been a great success; many people commented that they were relaxing. It seemed to stop small children running around – they were more interested in watching the fish.'

Goldfish – a good thing

▶

'The clinic has seen a 30 per cent increase in patient throughput. It's not surprising that the car park gets full. Sometimes there's a queue back out on to the road. There's going to be an accident one day.'

The car park isn't big enough

'King Arthur had a point! The shape of the table is vital to the success of the meeting – I think we should consider a round table, or at least a broad oval. These long boardroom tables make sensible discussion impossible. I can't hear Ken and they're chatting at the back.'

Change shape of table to round/broad oval

'I used to work for a hospital in the Midlands, luckily not one of those in Birmingham city centre because parking is a non-starter. All the furniture there was incredibly old, probably from the 50s or even before. But it was strong and solid and outlasted all the newer "cheap" stuff. Quality has to be a prime concern because it's cheaper in the long run.'

Must buy good quality – long-term saving

'Staff don't know how to use the programs or the system. Computer training was offered to all staff in 2013, and 50 courses were run. In 2014 it was 45, in 2011 it was just 20, and in 2016 it was 9, but new programs are coming in all the time and we expect them to learn by magic.'

Need to provide computer training

'Everyone in this team wants the new system; well, a couple of the administrators aren't too keen but they'll come around. Oh, and Tim is anti – but he always is. Everyone else is keen.'

Views are mixed about new system

Developing the skill

As we've seen, the essential skill is not the ability to write fast, but the ability to recognize what someone is talking about and identify the message. There are many everyday opportunities to develop this skill:

- Alone, for example in the car, listen to the news headlines and at the same time say aloud what they are about:
 - inflation figures;
 - riots in the Middle East;
 - bed shortages in the health service;
 - England's cricket victory;
 - bus crash;
 - football violence.
- As soon as you are confident of these, take it a stage forward and add in the crucial message:
 - inflation figures, up by 3 per cent;
 - riots in the Middle East, two deaths and many injured;
 - bed shortages in the health service, worries about A & E patients left on trolleys;
 - England's cricket victory, by eight runs with three overs to play;
 - bus crash, no one injured;
 - football violence, many arrests.
- Watch television drama or soap operas and, as you watch the scene, define what it is about and the key arguments: 'They're arguing about where to live: he wants to stay with his parents; she wants them to get their own flat.'
- Watch celebrity or sports interviews and do the same thing: 'He played football as a child; he was spotted by a sports coach at his local club.'

- Summarize back or 'reflect' what has been said to you: 'So when the machine didn't work you checked for paper jam, the paper stock and the toner cartridge.'

- Mentally summarize conversations around you: 'She enjoyed the group charter of a boat; he didn't – wasn't with a friendly group.'

Try to use good preparation and administration to avoid taking notes to verbal updates; ask the person giving the update to provide the information before the meeting. This also applies to information given at the start of a discussion. For example, an overview of a system problem that the group will go on to discuss. By getting the detail before the meeting, the minute-taker can just listen to that explanation and be ready to take notes when the discussion begins.

SUMMARY POINTS

- Find a way of taking notes that suits you.
- Listen for the points made (not the words spoken).
- Ignore the tone or manner of speech.
- Once you have a point noted, you don't need to write it again every time it's made.

9 Structuring notes

Even with the best chairperson and a well-disciplined committee, you are likely to find that the discussion jumps around within an agenda item. For most minute-takers, making sense of a discussion with many different aspects is a significant problem. Some of the time you can move around your notes as you take them and add information where it is relevant. On other occasions, your notes will follow the order of the discussion and need to be structured at the writing-up stage.

If you are to type the minutes in a time-efficient manner, it is essential that you do not type up your notes and then cut-and-paste them into minutes. Although this can work in the end, it is very time consuming and the information that is not needed tends to obscure the detail that should be included. In order to save time and improve the minutes, an extra stage is needed between the hand-written notes and the draft minutes that result from them.

Remember that minutes are a document in their own right and must be clear to an outsider with no knowledge of the topic.

Follow the agenda

Whatever numbering and headings appear on the agenda must also appear in the minutes. If you have numbered objectives on the agenda, these should be turned into headings for the minutes, but keep the same number. Figures 9.1 and 9.2 illustrate how this can be done.

5. **Visit of David Smith MP**
 5.1 To confirm timetable for visit
 5.2 To agree strategy for maximizing publicity
 5.3 To discuss security implications of visit

FIGURE 9.1 Objectives on the agenda

5. **Visit of David Smith MP**
 5.1 Timetable
 5.2 Publicity strategy
 5.3 Security implications

FIGURE 9.2 Headings on the minutes

If the meeting used a 'basic' agenda

If the agenda was very general, the minute-taker will have to take each subject within the agenda item and write it up, presenting the information grouped and in a logical order.

For example, if the committee discussed 'redecoration of canteen', their concerns will range through the amount of money to be spent; the colour scheme to be chosen; whether to replace furniture and, if so, with what; the lighting and so on. They are unlikely to deal with each and move on; rather it will be discussion that touches repeatedly on the different points. Actions will come as and when decided and will often be revisited and changed.

In the minutes, the discussion on 'redecoration of canteen' is likely to be divided into several subheadings, which can be done without affecting the continuity between the agenda and minute numbering.

If the meeting used a full agenda

By breaking up the discussion into smaller sections, the discussion becomes more structured, but even so, there will be different aspects to consider.

For example, one subsection of the discussion on redecorating the canteen was 'furniture'. Within that, the committee will discuss tables and chairs. The discussion on tables is likely to cover colour, material, shape, size. Again, the numbering and headings on the agenda are likely to be subdivided, either into headings or simply by using paragraphs (whichever is most appropriate).

During the discussion a participant might raise an aspect of the discussion that is relevant to the subject, but not listed on the agenda. For example, your agenda might show the item in Figure 9.3.

If at any time during the discussion on these points the subject of flooring is raised and discussed, it must be minuted because it is relevant. Wherever it is discussed, use the next free number within the main agenda item to minute it (see Figure 9.4).

If the subject is not on the agenda at all

Provided the item is relevant to the work of the group it should be minuted. If there is not a section where it can slot in, include it under 'Any other business'.

> 7. **Redecoration of canteen**
> 7.1 Budget
> 7.2 Colour scheme
> 7.3 Furniture
> 7.4 Lights

FIGURE 9.3 Extract from a full agenda

> 7. **Redecoration of canteen**
> 7.1 **Budget**
> In comparison with the rest of the fifth-floor renovation, the cost of the canteen redecoration...
> 7.2 **Colour scheme**
> The canteen is a light room and therefore...
> 7.3 **Furniture**
> The furniture must be in keeping with the general style and colour of the canteen and...
> 7.4 **Lights**
> Several staff have complained about the strip lights causing headaches...
> 7.5 **Flooring**
> The current flooring is in good condition and is a neutral colour...

FIGURE 9.4 Add the new item at the end of the planned and numbered items

Depth of minutes

Before you can turn your notes into minutes, you need an idea of how much depth you are to go into (in fact, it is best to know this before you take the notes). The amount of information to be included can be divided into four 'levels'. Note that all of these will have the same action, and may have the same introduction.

As an example: you are minuting a discussion in the health and safety committee meeting on what to do about the reception flooring which is slippery when wet. The agenda item was headed 'Reception flooring' and the action that resulted is, 'Rink Flooring to be asked to resurface reception with British Standard flooring before end-October.'

Level one

This is simply the decision and the action (see Figure 9.5).

6. **Reception Flooring**
The group discussed the slip hazard of the reception flooring and decided that it would be resurfaced with a non-slip coating.
Action: Rink Flooring to be asked to resurface reception with British Standard flooring before end-October." **Alex Kimble**, 23/9/16

FIGURE 9.5 Example level-one minute

There is another depth which is even shorter than level one – where you just note the actions. These are usually called action minutes; you might be asked to, '… just note the action'. If you are asked to do this, it is a good idea to clarify whether they really want a list of actions (or outcomes) or whether they want level one with the heading, the decision and the action.

Level two

This gives the reason(s) for the decision and/or more information about it (see Figure 9.6).

6. **Reception Flooring**
The group discussed the slip hazard of the reception flooring and decided that, as it became slippery when wet, it would be resurfaced with a non-slip coating.
Action: Rink Flooring to be asked to resurface reception with British Standard flooring before end-October. **Alex Kimble**, 23/9/16

FIGURE 9.6 Example level-two minute

The important thing to remember is that level-two minutes are all about what is happening, with no mention of any alternatives that were discussed but not taken forward. This is the most popular depth as they are clear, focussed and forward-moving.

Level three

This includes a simple mention of any alternatives that were considered (see Figure 9.7).

> 6. **Reception Flooring**
> The group discussed the slip hazard of the reception flooring which becomes slippery when wet. They considered purchasing warning signs to be put out during wet weather but decided that it would be resurfaced with a non-slip coating.
> *Action*: Rink Flooring to be asked to resurface reception with British Standard flooring before end-October. **Alex Kimble**, 23/9/16

FIGURE 9.7 Example level-three minute

In theory, level three is a good style because it does show that the discussion was wider than a simple 'go with the first idea'. However, simply mentioning an alternative often causes people to question how the alternative would have worked, why it was discounted, etc. It is also difficult to write up level-three minutes because once a subject is mentioned, it is tempting to give additional information about it and the minutes drift into level four.

Level four

This goes into detail on things that are not going to be taken forward (see Figure 9.8).

> 6. **Reception Flooring**
> The group discussed the slip hazard of the reception flooring which becomes slippery when wet. They considered purchasing warning signs to be put out during wet weather; these are easily and cheaply available, complying with current health and safety regulations but the group decided that the floor would be resurfaced with a non-slip coating.
> *Action*: Rink Flooring to be asked to resurface reception with British Standard flooring before end-October." **Alex Kimble**, 23/9/16

FIGURE 9.8 Example level-four minute

The committee discussed the use of a text-based system to remind patients of their appointment. They considered asking reception staff to do this using the type-to-text option on the booking system but were concerned about the time this would take and the risk of the need to text being overlooked. They agreed that the automated AppointAlert would be the most cost- and time-efficient approach. Outright purchase would give greater certainty over finance but there were concerns about the need for ongoing software updates which will incur unknown costs in the future. The cost of a technical support contract was around 20 per cent of the lease cost and the latest software update was 40 per cent of the current purchase price for the system. Leasing the system would spread the financial investment and ensure that the system is always maintained and up to date. It was therefore decided to take out the three-year contract in order to attract a 5 per cent discount.

FIGURE 9.9 A level-four minute

Level-four minutes give a full overview of the discussion but they are very lengthy and the ultimate decision and action often gets overshadowed by detail on options that are not being pursued. Look at Figure 9.9 (a minute of a discussion from a large clinical practice about introducing a text system to remind patients of their appointment). It has a good structure: the issue, each option and the final decision, but the reader tends to assume that each issue is 'the one', only to discover that they are wrong and have to mentally back-track. By the time the final option is reached, most readers have given up.

EXERCISE

Take the level-four minute in Figure 9.9 and turn it into a level-three minute (just mention the alternatives in the briefest form), then into a level-two minute (focus on what is being done) and finally a level-one minute (just the action).

EXERCISE MODEL ANSWER

Level three (mention what else considered)
The committee considered asking staff to text patients to remind them of their appointments but decided on the use of the automated AppointAlert. Outright purchase was considered but leasing the system would ensure the system is always maintained and up to date. It was therefore decided to take out the three-year contract in order to attract a 5 per cent discount.

Level two (what is being done)
The committee considered the use of AppointAlert to enable text reminders to be sent to patients to remind them of their appointments. Leasing the system would ensure the system is always maintained and up to date, and it was decided to take out the three-year contract in order to attract a 5 per cent discount.

Level one (decision only)
The committee decided to adopt a text-based reminder system and take out a three-year contract for AppointAlert.

Note: The action for this would be the same, irrespective of the depth of the minute.

If you are required to write level-four minutes, make good use of subheadings, bullet points and paragraphing. Figure 9.10 shows the AppointAlert discussion written up more clearly.

Note that the action and most of the introduction remains unchanged as the depth increases.

There is no rule about which level is most appropriate and you will find that you can seldom be rigidly consistent in the level you choose. The big break point is between levels two and three – it is

The committee discussed the use of a text-based system to remind patients of their appointment. They considered asking reception staff to do this using the type-to-text option on the booking system but were concerned about the time this would take and the risk of the text needing to be proofread.

They agreed that the automated AppointAlert would be the most cost- and time-efficient approach:

- Outright purchase would give greater certainty over finance, but there were concerns about the need for ongoing software updates which will incur unknown costs in the future. The cost of a technical support contract was around 20 per cent of the lease cost and the latest software update was 40 per cent of the current purchase price for the system.
- Leasing the system would spread the financial investment and ensure that the system is always maintained and up to date.

It was therefore decided to take out the three-year contract for AppointAlert in order to attract a 5 per cent discount.

FIGURE 9.10 A level-four minute with a more reader-friendly layout

level three that starts to include mention of things that are not going to be done. Most people seem to prefer level two so it is probably a good idea to prepare your minutes at that level and see what feedback you get.

Structuring your notes

Within an agenda item, the discussion is likely to jump around as individuals reintroduce their personal concerns or views. As minute-taker, you should ignore the order of the discussion and instead structure the minutes according to the order of the content.

Read through the notes in Figure 9.11, taken during an item on how to generate interest in the organization's suggestion scheme.

These notes are broadly in the order of:

- loss of interest;
- why it's happened;
- motivating staff to suggest;

> *Not many people making suggestions*
> *Only four last month*
> *Why? system stale*
> * no reason to bother*
> * no one wants to be the 'goody goody'*
>
> *Give up on it? Run for six years.*
> *Or encourage use: how?*
> * write-up in magazine*
> * an award – certificate*
> * financial reward*
> * a gift*
> *Money is the key*
> *How much? £5 – £50 – £20? £50*
> *For suggestions that are implemented*
> *Who pays? – whoever benefits*
> *Advertise the change? – noticeboards, e-mail*
> *When/how to give: party*
> * director*
> * by manager*
> * internal post*
> *Arrange with manager, can present it or just hand it over.*
> *Lots of money – too much?*
> *If not a £50 saving, then idea won't be implemented*
> *– must be an incentive*

FIGURE 9.11 Notes taken during a discussion on the future of the suggestion scheme

- money;
- how to advertise the new system;
- how to hand over the reward;
- money/motivating staff to suggest;
- advertising the new system.

As you can see there is some duplication. The most common way of dealing with this is to type up the notes and then start editing. To save time and improve the quality of the minutes, structure the notes before typing them up. Look at a suggested structure for the notes above (Figure 9.12).

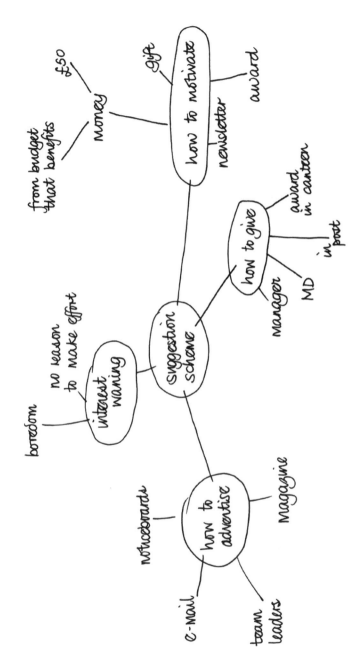

FIGURE 9.12 Discussion notes, structured into logical groups

The committee discussed the drop in support for the suggestion scheme. There was support for the system in principle and it was agreed that efforts should be made to generate more interest.

In order to encourage suggestions, it was decided to offer a financial reward for successful ideas, and agreed that £50 was an appropriate figure. This will come from whichever budget benefits from the saving.

The manager of successful staff members could arrange a presentation or simply pass the money on as deemed appropriate. In addition, the managing director would be informed so that a congratulatory note could be sent, and the idea would appear in the magazine.

Staff should be informed of the changes through the newsletter and posters on the noticeboards. Suggestions made after 31 May would be eligible for the payment.

Posters to be put up during w/c 22 May
Article to be inserted in May issue of newsletter

Action: **Tom Brind**
17 April 2017

FIGURE 9.13 A very detailed minute

Some minute-takers could produce the structure in Figure 9.12 in the meeting. Most would take notes as in Figure 9.11, then sort out the structure back in the office.

This structure has taken all the notes that could be used – a very detailed minute. If this was what was required, it could be written up as shown in Figure 9.13.

This minute is in the structure/order of: interest waning; how to motivate; how to give; telling staff.

For most purposes, only some of the information would be used to write a shorter minute. The structure would then look like the one in Figure 9.14.

A briefer minute would be written up as shown in Figure 9.15.

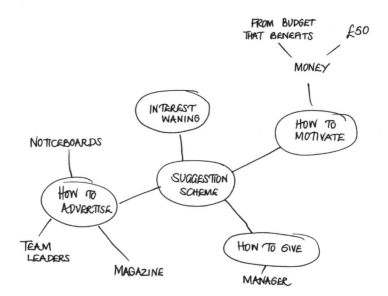

FIGURE 9.14 Structure for a briefer minute

The committe discussed the drop in support for the suggestion scheme. It was decided to offer a £50 reward for successful ideas, to come from whichever budget would benefit from the saving.

The money will be given by the relevant manager. The managing director would be informed so that a congratulatory note could be sent, and the idea would appear in the magazine.

Suggestions made after 31 May would be eligible for the payment.

Posters to be put up during w/c 22 May

Article to be inserted in May issue of newsletter

*Action: **Tom Brind***
17 April 2017

FIGURE 9.15 A brief minute

Using the structure

To use a structure like the one outlined above, note your subject in the centre of the space. Take each point you have noted and decide whether it is relevant. If it is, look to see whether it relates to a point that you already have. If it does, link the two. If it does not, start a new 'area'. This process is illustrated in Figure 9.16.

Structuring your notes like this will mean that you have the skeleton of the minute before you write, which saves considerable time in writing and editing. Also, interruptions won't cause you to lose your train of thought, as they could do if you are 'translating' your notes into sentences. In addition, as you go through the process you generally move from the wording in your notes (words they may have said) to your phrasing (a summary of their message). Type the minutes from your structure, referring to your notes when you need more detail.

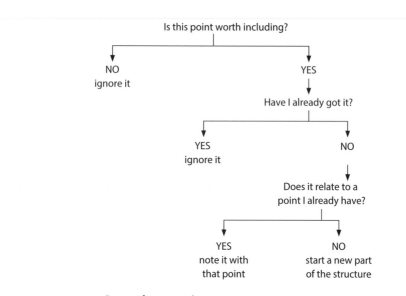

FIGURE 9.16 Process for structuring notes

If you have taken notes on a laptop

It is still possible to follow the system with notes taken on a laptop; the same principles can be followed electronically.

First save the notes as a new document so you always have the original to fall back on.

For each agenda item, insert a two-column table and cut and paste the notes into the left column. In the right column, note the relevant points. These can then be cut and pasted back into the minute and the table deleted. See Figure 9.17 for an example.

Not many people making suggestions Only four last month Why? system stale no reason to bother no one wants to be 'goody goody'	Interest waning
Give up on it? Run for six years Or encourage use – how: write up in magazine an award – certificate financial reward a gift	
Money is the key How much? £5 - £50 - £20? _£50_ For suggestions that are implemented	Pay money to motivate – £50 If implemented. From budget that benefits.
How advertise to staff – noticeboards, magazine	
Who pays? – whoever benefits When/how to give party director by manager internal post Arrange with manager, can present it or just hand over Can ask managers to tell staff about it	Advertise on notice- boards, magazine, through line managers Give by manager however liked
Lots of money – too much? If not a £50 saving then idea won't be implemented – must be an incentive	

FIGURE 9.17 From notes in the meeting to relevant points

The notes could then be written up as shown in Figure 9.18

Cut and paste from table
Interest waning

Pay money to motivate – £50
If implemented. From budget that benefits

Advertise on noticeboards, magazine, through line managers

Give by manager however liked

Put into an appropriate order
Interest waning

Pay money to motivate – £50
If implemented. From budget that benefits

Give by manager however liked

Advertise on noticeboards, magazine, through line managers

Type as minute
The group accepted that interest in the suggestion scheme was waning and agreed to try to motivate staff by paying £50 for suggestions that were implemented; payable from the budget that benefits. The money would be given by the individual's manager. It was decided to advertise this through the noticeboards, magazine and through line managers.

FIGURE 9.18 Process of moving from notes to minute

SUMMARY POINTS

- Although it is tempting to rush into typing up the minutes, time spent on sorting through your notes will save time later.

- Decide on the 'depth' of your minutes before you start deciding what is needed for the minutes as this will give you a filter to identify relevance.

- Break each discussion down into the aspects discussed and then write up the minutes in a logical structure (according to content).

- The headings and numbering on the agenda must be followed in the minutes.

10 Writing up the minutes

Minutes are not a record of what was said. They are a record of what was discussed.

Your minutes must show:

- who was at the meeting, and who could have been there (apologies/absent);
- that the previous minutes were approved (and amendments if necessary);
- the status of actions from previous meetings;
- the decisions that were made;
- the actions that resulted from those decisions.

Most groups also want a summary of the reasons for the decision that was made.

You can argue endlessly about the difference between the *notes* of a meeting and the *minutes* of a meeting. It is easiest to work on the basis that 'notes' are what you take in the meeting to enable you to write 'minutes' which is the document published to the group. The minutes can be long or short, formal or informal, etc but if they are the document that is circulated to participants they are 'minutes'. In fact it doesn't matter what you call them so long as you have the distinction clear in your mind: one for your use, the other for the participants' information and ongoing record.

Do you have time to sit back at work and read a magazine? It's very unlikely that you do, but minutes can waste just as much time and probably more. If the meeting finishes at 11.00 and you go back, make a coffee then do the minutes, you will probably have them done by 12.30. If you spend that time on the messages/e-mails then go for lunch before doing the minutes, they will probably take at least two hours. Leave them until the next day or so and the time taken is likely to be three or four hours. Put them off for a week or so and it's probably a day's work. You'd be spending eight hours on a job you could have done in an hour or so…that's a lot of magazine reading! Or more likely doing other work, taking a proper lunch break or going home on time.

There is the added benefit that a fast turnaround of minutes reflects well on your efficiency and, if you need to ask for help, doing so promptly looks considerably more professional than contacting people after a few days or weeks (when they won't be able to remember either).

Speeding up the process

Prepare templates or master documents

For each meeting set up a master document with the margins set up, heading, the list of those who should attend and so on. All you will then have to do is cut and paste the names to 'present', 'apologies' or 'absent', copy across the main agenda headings and make sure all are the correct size, bold, etc.

Inserting variable information

You can save time by setting up your master document with variable information (such as the date) replaced with a symbol: # is an

easy one to choose because it is near the return key. Write a macro to find the # symbol (CTRL # is a simple one to use). This means that every time you type CTRL #, the cursor will jump to the next # sign and highlight it.

For each meeting, set up a master minutes document with the layout information in place (header, footer, margins, tab stops, etc). Type in the information that is standard for that meeting (name of group, names/job titles, fixed headings). Decide how you will present the minutes (a table, an action column, full width text with an action box). Again, set up a master that can be cut and pasted as needed. As you do this, type # wherever variable information will be entered (date, time, venue, action, name/date). This can also be done for regular content ('The minutes of the meeting held on # were approved'). For each #, make sure that it is in the correct size and highlighting so that when you get to each one, the text is as you want it.

This may take some time to do, but the time saving is significant when you use the template. Open it and save it in the normal way and copy the agenda headings across as a block, delete the information that isn't needed and edit the formatting ready for the minutes. Return to the top of the document and use your macro to insert the variable text; if using an action box, note where actions were given and copy it into the minutes as necessary and then type up the minutes.

Writing the minutes

Remember that your minutes are not your notes typed up. Your notes are there to inform the minutes but not to be them.

Before the meeting, enter the 'administrative' information (date, time, etc) and fill in any reports/information items or background to discussion that you have received as part of your preparation.

Remember to check that what you were given in advance reflects what was said on the day – you may need to edit. This saves time after the meeting and also makes the minutes less daunting when you open up a document that is already underway.

After the meeting, return to the document, cut and paste the names into the correct headings to reflect attendance and complete the relatively simple sections such as changes to the minutes and their approval, update on actions and declarations of interest.

When it comes to writing the decision items, it is important to avoid just typing up your notes and then editing them into minutes. This takes a long time and risks including information that is duplicated or irrelevant. It also tends to make the structure of the minute reflect the order of the discussion which seldom leads to a clear summary. Create a structure for each minute as outlined in the previous chapter and use that to type the finished summary.

The IRDA structure

This structure is very useful for a minute which results in a decision and action. It stands for: Issue, Reason/Rationale, Decision, and Action. These headings are not used, but they underpin the structure of the minute: the current situation or problem, why they made the decision they made, what that decision was and how it will happen.

The sections can be written up in any order as the structure is in place. It is generally helpful to write up the issue first (to clarify what you are writing about) and then move to the decision (so you know where you are going with the minute). Having got those in place, ask yourself *why* they made that decision (to give yourself the reason) and then define the action. See Figures 10.1–10.5 as an example.

Question: 'What is the issue under discussion?'

5. Reception floor
[Issue]
 The group discussed the risk factors relating to the reception area as there
 have been four reports of falls.
[Reason]

[Decision]

[Action]

FIGURE 10.1 The IRDA structure – Issue

Question: 'What are they going to do about it?'

Reception floor
[Issue]
 The group discussed the risk factors relating to the reception area as there
 have been four reported falls.
[Reason]

[Decision]
 It was agreed to resurface the reception floor with a non-slip coating.
[Action]

FIGURE 10.2 The IRDA structure – Decision

Question: 'Why did they make that decision?'

Reception floor
[Issue]
 The group discussed the risk factors relating to the reception area as there
 have been four reported falls.
[Reason]
 The floor can be slippery when wet.
[Decision]
 It was agreed to resurface the reception floor with a non-slip coating.
[Action]

FIGURE 10.3 The IRDA structure – Reason

Question: 'How is it going to happen?'

Reception floor
[Issue]
 The group discussed the risk factors relating to the reception area as there
 have been four reported falls.
[Reason]
 The floor can be slippery when wet.
[Decision]
 It was agreed to resurface the reception floor with a non-slip coating.
[Action]
 Three quotes to be obtained for a clear surface that meets the required British
 Standard. **Michael Readwin**
 23 June 2017

FIGURE 10.4 The IRDA structure – Action

Reception floor
The group discussed the risk factors relating to the reception area; there have
been four reported falls as the floor can be slippery when wet. It was agreed to
resurface the reception floor with a non-slip coating.

 Action: Three quotes to be obtained for a clear surface that meets the
 required British Standard. **Michael Readwin**
 23 June 2017

FIGURE 10.5 The IRDA structure – finished minute

In some minutes, the 'issue' is part of the reason for the 'decision'.
The reception floor minute could be written as:

Reception floor
The floor can be slippery when wet and there have been four reported falls. It was
agreed to resurface the reception floor with a non-slip coating.

In a longer minute, each section might be a paragraph. In other situations the paragraphs can merge: the 'issue' and 'reason' might form one, or the 'reason' and 'decision' another. The 'action' must always be a separate paragraph.

IRDA FOR MORE DETAILED MINUTES

If more detailed minutes are required, it is simple to insert the extra information to make them into level three or four (see Chapter 9 for information on the depths of minutes).

For level-three minutes (those that just mention the alternatives that were discussed), these can be included before the 'reason'.

Reception floor
The group discussed the risk factors relating to the reception area as there have been four reports of people falling as the floor can be slippery when wet. The possibility of putting out warning signs in wet weather was considered but it was agreed to resurface the reception floor with a non-slip coating.

If level-four minutes are required (which detail alternatives that were discounted), build in the details at the same point.

Reception floor
The group discussed the risk factors relating to the reception area as there have been four reports of people falling as the floor can be slippery when wet. The possibility of putting out warning signs in wet weather was considered but there were concerns about when and how reception staff would make the decision to use these. It was agreed to resurface the reception floor with a non-slip coating.

HAVE A GO AT THE IRDA APPROACH

Take your notes for an item where there is a decision and an action.

1 Summarize the issue they discussed:

2 Define the decision, and what they agreed to do about it:

3 State why they decided to do that:

4 What does someone have to do to make it happen:

These should then be typed up with the decision then action at the end; the reason before that and the issue first.

If you can't type the minutes for a few days

Spend a few minutes reading your notes at the end of the meeting

Avoid returning to your desk until you have spent five minutes or so reading your notes, editing and adding bits. Once you return to the phone messages and an overflowing in-tray, your memory will start to fade.

Highlight any amendments to the previous minutes and the update on actions. For each agenda item, mark the decision and the action (highlight pens come in useful here). Delete anything which turned out to be unnecessary with hindsight and mark where discussion on an item took place in different parts of the meeting; finally, put a clear mark between agenda items.

Use a dictating machine

You can go over your notes with a dictating machine. Do not try to dictate as though to a secretary, just add your verbal thoughts and comments to your written notes. The minutes can then be typed up from the mix of notes and audio. It can help to define the decision and action for each item as a list which can then be incorporated into the minutes when they are typed later. The Dragon dictation system can be invaluable for this as your audio thoughts will be on your computer as a typed document when you do get to type them.

If you need help

There is no shame in not understanding (or being able to keep up with fast-paced discussion), but you will need to ask for help if you have gaps in your notes. If someone has given factual information (figures, dates, description of a problem or system) then ring or e-mail to ask them to repeat the information for you. However, if it is discussion that you missed, you can only ask the chairperson for guidance because if you asked the person promoting an idea you would get a different answer than if you asked the manager who would have to fund it... or the manager who tried it before and it failed... or the person who will have to staff it... or change their system to incorporate it.

Get the chairperson's approval

The chairperson is responsible for the minutes (even though you have done the work) and must approve them before dispatch. This serves as a double-check on what you have written.

Don't take amendments until the next meeting

Once you send out the minutes you might get corrections phoned or e-mailed to you. These can be noted, but the minutes should not be amended until the next meeting, because other people may have different views of what went on and all participants should have the opportunity to know about, and approve, changes. You will also open the minutes to manipulation if changes are made without the knowledge of all and you might find you have contradictory changes where people agree it's wrong, but not what it should read.

SUMMARY POINTS

- Work done before the meeting on creating templates will save time and stress afterwards.

- Go over notes before you return to the workplace to tidy them, define acronyms, etc.

- Type the minutes soon after the meeting; ideally, immediately after.

- Structure your minutes so they summarize the issue and define the decision/action.

11 The minutes

Minutes, like all business writing, have changed in style over the years. As with letters and reports, the drive is towards plain English with short sentences and paragraphs, and a clear, reader-friendly style. Your minutes are likely to be read by one or more of three groups of readers:

- The current group (who may well use them to fill in gaps in concentration).
- Someone in the future who remembers something from the past and needs more information.
- An 'investigator' in the future who is looking into something that has gone wrong.

In the case of the second and third groups, by the time they need information, those who were part of the decision-making may have left or be unable to remember what went on at the meeting. The minutes are the only record of what was decided and how it was put into place (or not).

Minutes have become shorter. In most cases two pages that are read are preferred to ten pages that are filed. There are, however, still some conventions that are followed; generally, these have survived because they are sensible, serving a practical purpose.

Heading

The heading of the minutes should follow the style of the agenda, whether that be the traditional paragraph style or the more modern centred layout.

The agenda showed the planned start and finish times; the minutes should reflect the actual start and finish times. The agenda gave enough detail about the venue to get the participants to the right room. The minutes can be less detailed – whether it was Room 3 or Room 4 is unlikely to matter.

Who attended

The names at the start of a set of minutes are often thought of as 'who was there?' In fact the priority is 'who are the group?' They are simply arranged according to whether or not they attended, and in what capacity.

For a group that meets regularly, there are seven headings that can be used. Few need all seven but the order of those used should remain the same.

Present

The names of those who make up the group are shown. The chairperson is usually listed first with the others following in alphabetical order. Avoid any order of hierarchy, or differentiation like clinical/managerial or uniformed/civilian, as this highlights differences between members of the group that are usually discouraged.

It is advisable to put the people in context by giving their job title, and the department or organization represented. For example, Helen Graham might be attending the meeting to represent the finance department, the Manchester office, the organization, the union, women returners to work, etc. Just giving her name under 'present' is not really enough to be useful to future readers.

Present

Charles Evans	Finance
Sue Graham	A & E
Alan Harris	Day Care Unit
Andrew Marks	Communications
Represented by Ann Jakes	
Amanda Watts	Elderly Care

FIGURE 11.1 Show where a member sent a substitute

Usually names are listed as first name and surname. It is not necessary to show the initials in brackets unless they are not obvious; even then it is better to use full names for action points and no names in the minutes.

Where someone has sent a representative or substitute, the name of the intended participant should be listed under 'present' but it should be noted that they were represented by X (see Figure 11.1).

Representatives can present a problem for the minute-taker because the person wasn't there, but their views were given. The issue here is demonstrating 'for the record' who was responsible for the decisions made, and there is no one simple answer. This is best illustrated by an example (Sally Smith is the committee member and Tom Turner is the person she sent on her behalf):

- If Tom was sent to simply watch and report back, he should be listed under 'Observer'. You could note 'on behalf of Sally Smith', or their department.

- If Tom attends in his own right (because Sally wasn't there), putting forward his own views and opinions, he should be listed as 'In attendance'. In this case though, he is not *representing* the committee member as his views are his own.

- If Tom is sent by Sally to represent her, he is, by definition, there to give Sally's views, argue her corner and generally delegated to 'be her'. This is where the problem lies:

- If you list Sally under 'Present' it would not be true or accurate as she wasn't there, hence why it is important to show 'Represented by Tom Turner'.

- If you list Tom under 'In attendance' it would not be accurate because he wasn't there as himself; he was there to be Sally, giving her views and committing to decisions on her behalf. You can, of course put 'Representing Sally Smith' after his name but there is the risk that in the future, someone looking to see if Sally was there would simply look down the 'Present' list and find that she was not when, in fact, her views had been put to the meeting and, through Tom, she was responsible for the decision that was made.

- Sally should not be listed under 'Apologies' because, three years down the line, someone looking for her name would see she wasn't there when, in fact, her views were put to the group via Tom. It would look as though a decision was made without input from a particular department.

- The key point here is whether Sally influenced and took responsibility for the committee's decision, and if she did, she should be listed under 'Present'. In the representative situation, she does this by delegating to Tom; so it is shown as 'Sally Smith, represented by Tom Turner'.

For some meetings, there is guidance for this laid down in the terms of reference. Ultimately, what matters is that it will be clear in the future who influenced and who made the decisions.

For a one-off or general meeting, those who attended are generally listed under 'Attendees' or 'Attended'. This indicates a one-off meeting, whereas 'Present' is used to describe a core group.

In attendance

For those who are attending on a one-off basis, generally the name and department or organization are shown. You can also choose to

In attendance

Desmond Barnham	Communications	
Sandy McPherson	J M Albany Ltd	item 9
Andy Morris	Secretariat	to item 6
Corinne Thorney	IT, Head Office	from item 3
Mel Wilson	Newman & Co	items 4–8

FIGURE 11.2 Information that should be included under 'In attendance'

show when they attended. This is done by noting the item number after the name. If you do this, those with no number are assumed to have attended the whole meeting. An example is shown in Figure 11.2.

The minute-taker is listed under 'In attendance' with either 'minute-taker' or 'secretary' after the name. Although it is a minor difference, minute-taker implies that you took the notes and typed them up, whereas secretary indicates that you organized the agenda, booked the room, etc.

The key difference between 'Present' and 'In attendance' comes historically from the days when decisions were proposed, seconded and voted upon. Those listed in 'Present' could vote and thus were responsible for the outcomes. Although a vote is seldom taken, the principle remains – those who can be held responsible, the committee or group, are listed under 'Present'. This is why the minute-taker is listed in 'In attendance'. If you are a member of the group who also takes minutes, your name should be in 'Present' but put minutes after your name to indicate your dual role.

Any actions from the meeting *must* be the responsibility of a group member, whether they were to do something themselves or make sure that someone else does something. Someone listed under 'In attendance' cannot be given an action. This can lead to problems with some board meetings where the voting members are listed under 'Present' but actions tend to be the responsibility

of senior members of the organization who attend the meetings and contribute to the discussions. In this situation, use the heading 'Present' but sub-divide the people into 'Voting members' and 'Non-voting members'. That way it is clear who is a regular attendee, who informs and influences decisions and who makes those decisions.

Observer

Observers are those who are only there to watch. They are usually learning or shadowing a participant. Occasionally they may be there for audit purposes. In the case of a public meeting, members of the public are listed here because they do not take an active part in the decision-making process. They do not have to be named, but can be listed as 'Members of the public (27)'. If there are reporters present they can be listed as either 'The press (3)' or with the publications detailed.

Apologies

For a regular meeting or one where specific people have been invited, people who do not attend the meeting fall into two groups: 1) those who have apologized; and 2) those who do not turn up.
Apologies can be made:

- when the date of the meeting is set during the previous meeting (nothing to record on that meeting's minutes; include under 'Apologies' on the minutes of the meeting that is missed);
- during the intervening period to the chairperson or secretary;
- on the day via a message from a colleague who is attending.

These members are listed under 'Apologies'.

Absent

Anyone you expect, but who does not turn up, should be listed under 'Absent'. It is important not just to leave off the names of those who don't attend. You are providing a record of who attended a meeting and a broader record of who was involved in that group at that time. Using 'Absent' gives you a complete list for administrative purposes and means the record is complete (and makes a comment about those whose commitment is questionable). Alternative headings are 'Did not attend' or 'Not present'.

For a meeting that is open to a wide group of people, for example all nursing staff within the hospital, only note those who have apologized. The others can be left off.

Invited but did not attend

This is for those who were invited to the meeting as a one-off (would have been shown under 'In attendance'), but did not attend.

Copy

If the minutes are circulated to any individual or group other than those involved in the meeting (and listed above), they should be detailed in this section. This might mean giving names or general groups (eg 'All team leaders') or perhaps the most general of all, 'Noticeboards'. Other headings for this could be 'For information', 'Circulation', 'Distribution', or similar.

LAYOUT

Although the heading 'Apologies' is used on the agenda, the names are often included in a list at the start of the minutes, after those who are present (see Figure 11.3). If you plan to do this, do not number 'Apologies' on the agenda or your numbering will be one place awry.

Present			In attendance	
Helen Pratt	Finance	(chair)	Frank Moss	Security item 8
Mark Delby	Marketing		Tina Parker	Minute-taker
Marion Fowkes	Finance			
Susannah Lewis	Sales		**Apologies**	
Roger Oswald	Marketing		Sulima Begg	Administration
Brian Winner	Finance			
Nick Wordsley	Administration		**Absent**	
Lizzie Young	Sales		Mary King	Sales

FIGURE 11.3 Example layout for including 'Apologies' as part of the listing at the top of the minutes

If you would rather number 'Apologies' on the agenda, start your minutes with this as the first item and include the names as two separate sentences (or paragraphs, if necessary), one for 'Apologies' and one for 'Absent' (see Figure 11.4).

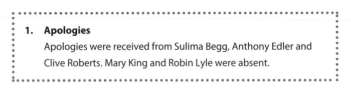

1. **Apologies**
 Apologies were received from Sulima Begg, Anthony Edler and Clive Roberts. Mary King and Robin Lyle were absent.

FIGURE 11.4 Example of layout including 'Apologies' as part of the text

QUORUM

The quorum is the number of the group who must be present for the meeting to take place. It might be a simple number or it may be more prescriptive; for example, laying down that a certain number must hold a particular role or qualification. This will be laid down in the terms of reference and it should be shown in the minutes that the meeting was 'quorate'. This is just a simple line before the first minute to show that, 'The meeting was quorate.'

If the quorum is not reached, the chairperson should decide what to do. This may mean abandoning the meeting or deferring some items (usually those involving expenditure). Again, the criteria will be laid down in the terms of reference for the group. Whatever is decided should be clearly minuted.

Introduction

It is unusual to see any introduction in the minutes. This is usually just the chairperson getting the meeting off to a businesslike start. If it is planned to use this as a more significant section, it should be on the agenda and should be minuted. If there is no intention to minute it, but something relevant is said that cannot go elsewhere, start the minutes with a paragraph to cover it, using no numbering or heading. That way the numbering and headings will remain correct.

Declarations of interest

Note any that are made, and what happened as a result.

The alternatives are usually that the person:

- resigned from the group;
- left the meeting;
- left the meeting for that item;
- stayed in the room but did not contribute;
- contributed but left the room for the decision;
- contributed to the discussion and decision.

This would be minuted on the lines of:

- Toby Ralph is part of the consortium that will be bidding for the supply of the filtration equipment; it was agreed he would leave the meeting for item six.

- Toby Ralph is part of the consortium that will be bidding for the supply of the filtration equipment; it was agreed he would not contribute to item six.

- Toby Ralph is part of the consortium that will be bidding for the supply of the filtration equipment; it was agreed he would contribute to the discussion, but would leave the meeting for the decision.

- Toby Ralph is part of the consortium that will be bidding for the supply of the filtration equipment; it was agreed this would cause no conflict of interest.

Someone can communicate a lot non-verbally, so the minutes should make it clear whether the person left the room or abstained (stayed in the room but didn't contribute).

Committee business

Any items raised under 'Committee business' should be minuted in the same style and layout as main agenda items.

If a more descriptive heading has been used on the agenda, this should also be used on the minutes. There may be guidance in the terms of reference for how items relating to the group should be dealt with, so the minutes may need to demonstrate that this guidance was followed.

Minutes of the previous meeting

It is important to confirm that the minutes of the previous meeting were accepted as this is where they become 'the minutes', or that the group wanted particular changes. Because of the importance of this, if the chairperson forgets to ask the group if they approve the minutes, the minute-taker should interrupt to ask, 'Should I record that the minutes are approved?'

If the minutes are correct

There are a number of variations that are acceptable:

- The minutes of the meeting held on [date] were approved.
- The minutes of the meeting held on [date] were accepted.
- The minutes of the meeting held on [date] were accepted as an accurate record.
- The minutes of the meeting held on [date] were signed.

If you have given the date of the last meeting in the heading ('Minutes of the meeting held on [date]'), the wording shown will change to 'The minutes of the previous meeting were…'

For higher-level meetings, you might want to name the group as well as reference the date, so it would read, 'The minutes of the executive board meeting held on [date] were approved.'

If there are errors

You can use a subheading of 'Amendments' and put any changes after this, or merely start with the first heading that contained an error (see Figure 11.5). Avoid putting 'changed from…to…' as this tends to muddle the reader. When all changes have been noted, type 'The minutes of the meeting held on [date] were subsequently approved…'

There is no need to send out a corrected set of minutes – most people file both or the wrong one!

Make sure that the file copy is left corrected for those that follow. You might want to leave a note of the minutes that were circulated and subsequently changed (with the changes shown).

3.0 **Minutes of the previous meeting**

3.1 **Car park**
The islands will be raised '10 cm above ground level'.

3.2 **Reception flooring**
Second sentence to be replaced with:
The flooring would not have an obvious pattern such as the current design incorporating the logo. A muted pattern that allows the appearance of solid colour would be advisable to reduce the appearance of dirt.

3.3 **Renovation of storage sheds**
The deadline for completion of the renovation is 'December 2017'.

The minutes of the meeting held on [date] were subsequently approved.

FIGURE 11.5 Example layout for correcting previous minutes

Signing minutes

Minutes are signed as extra proof that everyone at the table agreed to their accuracy. Although seldom done these days, it is worth considering in case of future dispute. The chairperson should sign them on the front cover or last page, and every other page should be initialled. The minutes of the meeting will say, 'Minutes of the meeting held on [date] were signed as an accurate record.'

Matters arising (or updates on actions)

As discussed earlier, 'Matters arising' is often taken up with participants arguing over something already decided in a previous meeting or by individuals going into great detail of *how* they completed the action. Neither is required for the minutes.

Text is acceptable under 'Matters arising', but only when it is worthy of inclusion in its own right; for example, when an aspect

4. **Matters arising**

 4.1 **Car park barrier** (3.4/03.17)
 The car park barrier has been repaired and painted, using reflective paint.

 4.2 **Publicity for David Smith's visit** (5.2)
 The press releases have been sent to all local papers. Publication is not expected until the week of the visit.

 4.3 **Outdoor smoking area** (6)
 Because of the lack of people using the area in favour of the car park, it was agreed to clean the area and then leave it for storage for six months before decoration.
 H Wheatley
 24 November 2017

 4.5 **Canteen chairs** (7.2)
 Action not taken due to announcement of merger and uncertainty about the future of the site.

 4.6 **Delivery standards** (8.2)
 Action not yet taken. **D Simmonds**
 31 August 2017

FIGURE 11.6 Example layout for 'Matters arising', giving minimal text

of an action point needs consideration but was not discussed during the original meeting. Most of the time you should minute the true purpose of 'Matters arising' – to confirm that actions that were agreed have been taken or if not, what is to be done about it (see Figure 11.6).

Where actions relate to items which are already on the agenda

There are often agenda items which are carried forward from one meeting to the next, often involving actions. If you are minuting these, leave the relevant actions out of matters arising (or include them with a note that they are 'included in item X below'). For each

main agenda item, start off with the outstanding actions before moving on to the current discussion.

By using an agenda with the actions listed and these options in the minutes, every action that is agreed will be checked up on, confirmed or if necessary taken forward in a managed way, and this is recorded in the minutes. The minutes will fulfil their role as an 'audit trail'.

Where the whole meeting is matters arising

A whole meeting can be matters arising, usually for project-planning types of meetings. The minutes for these are likely to be in sections that relate to the project (see Figure 11.7), and each participant will confirm actions and raise current concerns.

11. **Launch Party**

 11.1 **Matters arising**
 Guest list
 The guest list has been drawn up and invitations sent.
 Press coverage
 Invitations have been sent to local papers and trade press.

 11.2 **Invitations to staff from other offices**
 The committee discussed extending invitations to senior management from all regional offices. In the interests of maximizing communications throughout the group, it was suggested that seniority was not a factor and that although one senior manager should be invited, a number of other invitations should be sent to each office.

 It was agreed to invite each regional manager and two other staff from each office. A letter to the manager to suggest colleagues from different departments would be preferred.

 Ceri Jones
 25 October 2017

FIGURE 11.7 Example matters arising incorporated in minutes

These concerns will be discussed and new actions may arise. If this is the case, for each heading start with the relevant actions and confirm their status before moving on to new discussion.

Using an action log

If you track actions through an action log (more detail in Chapter 12), it is important that the minutes demonstrate that the group knew which actions were completed and which hadn't been done. This can be achieved by minuting, 'The group reviewed the action log; actions 24, 26–31 and 33 were completed.' The minutes should show that the group also knew where actions hadn't been completed and what was to be done about them. So actions 25 and 32 would have subheadings in the minutes with the heading from the previous minutes and a note of their current status and next step towards completing the action.

Information items

These are the items that are to be received only – not for discussion. A report or update that precedes a discussion will be dealt with as a main agenda item, but the guidelines for minuting it are the same.

Written reports should always be circulated with the agenda so that participants can read them beforehand. It is not only the minute-taker who will struggle with a report – only those with a good understanding of the subject will be able to follow, and many participants just switch off.

Where the report is circulated with the agenda

There is no need to summarize what is said, as everyone will have a copy. It can be worded along the lines of:

- The committee received the finance director's report.
- The committee received the finance report.
- The finance director gave a report on the third quarter.

Make sure that you keep a file copy that is filed with the minutes.

Where the report is tabled (given out on the day)

The minutes should read as above; a copy can be attached for non-attenders.

If the minutes are published on the internet or an intranet and readers will not have access to the papers, include a brief summary in the minutes. Create a standard cover sheet including a summary section that can be copied to the minutes.

Where the report is verbal

Unless you have excellent shorthand there is not much chance of keeping up with reports because they tend to be fast and factual, often delivered in the rather flat style of reading aloud. You should either: ask the person to give you a copy and attach it to the minutes; or ask the person to give you a few-line summary for the minutes.

If you have to note the report

If there is no option but to note the report, cover only the briefest detail, usually what was talked about. For example, the minutes of a 10-minute report are shown in the following box.

> The team received a report on the experimental use of temporary sales staff, detailing the cost of the programme (£8,400), the benefits of short-term staff and the problems that resulted. The use of temporary staff will not be continued.

Main agenda items

Minutes must follow the order, numbering and headings of the agenda, but extra headings can be used providing the numbering remains the same. See the chapter on structuring notes for more information. If you have numbered objectives on your agenda, these should be presented as headings on the minutes, with the same number. For example:

> Agenda: 8.3 To agree format of advertisement
> Minutes: 8.3 Advertisement

The style of minutes has changed, and continues to do so. Along with the drive towards shorter, plain English writing has come a preference for a slightly less formal style. That is not the same as saying that minutes should be casual. The writing is still business-like, but many minute-takers prefer to focus on what is being discussed (factual minutes) rather than on what the committee did (traditional style). Both styles are 'correct'; the choice should be based on the preference of the chairperson and the committee (and, of course, the minute-taker).

Traditional minutes

Traditional minutes report what the committee did (see Figure 11.8). They are written in the past tense, looking back to what happened at the meeting. The phrasing depends on what happened. Consider these examples:

- The Training Manager explained that the second 'Investors in People' visit had been postponed.
- It was reported that the second 'Investors in People' visit had been postponed.

The commitee discussed the possibility of a branch falling on the temporary building. It was suggested that the building should not be sited so near the boundary, but no other location could be found. It was agreed to ask a tree surgeon to advise on the state of the trees and then discuss the location in the light of his comments.

Advice on condition of trees and risk to building
to be discussed with Ark Woodland Care **Nigel Hamlyn**
20 October 2017

FIGURE 11.8 Example minute in traditional style

- The committee heard that the second 'Investors in People' visit had been postponed.
- The committee discussed the postponement of the second 'Investors in People' visit.
- It was suggested that the commitment to 'Investors in People' may be weakening.
- The committee agreed that the commitment to 'Investors in People' was as strong as ever.

Factual or reporting minutes

Factual minutes report on the situation as it was discussed (see Figure 11.9). They are written in the appropriate tense and, again,

There is a possibility of a branch falling on the temporary building. As no other location can be found, a tree surgeon will be asked to advise on the state of the trees. The location can then be discussed.

Advice on condition of trees and risk to building
to be discussed with Ark Woodland Care **Nigel Hamlyn**
20 October 2017

FIGURE 11.9 Example minute in factual style

> - Risk of branch falling on temporary building.
> - No other location available.
> - Tree surgeon's opinion to be obtained before further discussion on location.
> *Action: Ask Ark Woodland Care for advice on condition of trees and risk to building.* **Nigel Hamlyn**
> 20 October 2017

FIGURE 11.10 Bullet minutes

the phrasing depends on what was discussed. Consider these examples:

- The second 'Investors in People' visit has been postponed.
- Commitment to 'Investors in People' may be weakening.
- Commitment to 'Investors in People' is as strong as ever.

Sometimes facts/reporting minutes are presented as bullet points; usually the instruction to the minute-taker is, 'Just take bullet points.' An example is shown as Figure 11.10.

Any other business

Items taken under 'Any other business' should be minuted in the same style and format as the main agenda items. Give each a number and subheading under the main heading of 'Any other business'.

Beware irrelevant items

People will often take the chance of a captive audience to give out information or discuss things that are relevant to the individuals concerned, but not to the reason they are meeting at that time; in other words, issues that are outside the terms of reference or objectives for the group. These should not form part of the minutes. If it is necessary to circulate the information, it should be done as a separate note.

Items deferred to next meeting

Where the group do not have the time or necessary information to discuss an item, it will usually be put on the agenda for the next meeting. If this is a one-off, just minute the heading and note that it was deferred. If there are several items, you can use a heading of 'Items deferred to next meeting' and list them.

Items referred to another group

This should be dealt with in the same way as items deferred to the next meeting.

Date of next meeting

The date, time and place of the next meeting should be noted. If the meetings are set some time in advance, list the next few meetings.

It is also helpful to give a deadline for the receipt of agenda items (usually about eight days before the meeting) and a contact name and phone number/e-mail for agenda items, apologies, etc (see Figure 11.11).

Date of next meeting

The next meeting will be held at 11.15 am on 23 June 2017 in Room 7. Agenda items to be received by 16 June (Sue Thomas, x–2458, sue.thomas@marshalls.co.uk).

FIGURE 11.11 Example wording for 'Date of next meeting'

Close of meeting

If you have not shown the closing time as part of the heading, close the minutes with, 'The meeting closed at [time].'

Common questions about minutes

Do I include historical or background information?

At the start of a discussion, someone may begin by explaining the history of an issue. Quite often this is uninvited and, although relevant to the subject, is not necessarily of great interest. This should not be minuted. However, if that information is given because a large part of the group are not aware of it and need to know in order to discuss the subject, it can be minuted if you wish. Make sure it is a separate paragraph so that those who know already can easily skip it.

Do not fall into the trap of putting information in minutes because they will be read by those not at the meeting. If outsiders need information to understand the minutes, they should ask the chairperson. Once you start making the minutes full and complete for every reader you will have a small book for each meeting.

Do I name names?

No! Minutes are not a record of what was said, they are a record of what was discussed – they are subject-based, not speech-based. If you name names you will find that:

- some people won't stop talking because they want their names in the minutes;
- some people won't contribute because they don't want people to see that they expressed a particular view;
- someone will say, 'I didn't say that' when they see the minutes;
- someone else will say, 'you haven't got my point about X';
- several people will make the same point in a meeting – the decision about who to allocate it to is highly subjective;
- if you minute, 'Diane Merton said X', it is unclear whether she alone held that view, a few agreed or everyone shared the opinion;
- (most importantly) it makes the minutes difficult to understand! (See Figure 11.12.)

Almost a transcript, not minutes (speech-based)	Minutes (subject-based)
Clinic staffing	**Clinic staffing**
SM raised the issue of staffing for the new clinic and suggested a maximum of three nurses would be required for each session. BP suggested that a full-time secretary/receptionist would also be needed. SM suggested that in order to be as 'family friendly' as possible the nursing posts should be flexible hours, RS disagreed, saying this would have an impact on the continuity of the patient/nurse relationship. DI felt that as the clinic times would fall within normal working hours the administrative post could be one full-time person. SM suggested this was not necessary and a 25 hour week would cover the workload. She added there would also not be a problem with holidays and sickness cover as this could be arranged through other health centre staff. DI detailed the level of the workload and SM accepted that a full-time post was required. RS returned to the question of the nurses' hours, Sally Munro explained the importance of adhering to the 'family friendly' policy. BP suggested that the existing arrangements work well and DI confirmed that there has been no problem in switching shifts where necessary. SM accepted this was in line with the policy.	The group discussed staffing for the new clinic. It was agreed that three nurses were required for each session. It was decided that the current arrangements for nursing hours would be carried over from the existing clinic and this was in line with the 'family friendly' policy. There would be one full-time administrative/reception post.

FIGURE 11.12 Writing subject-based minutes

It can seem difficult to remove the names when the person is giving a report or update; every paragraph can start with 'X reported', 'X advised', 'X added', 'X emphasized', etc.

FIGURE 11.13 Removing names from updates

This can be avoided by putting the name of the person giving the report after the heading and then minuting just the points that were made. See Figure 11.13 for an example.

What 'person' do I use?

Minutes must always be written in the third person; that is, no reference to 'I', 'we' or 'you', 'your', etc. The common problem is with 'our' and vague references. In the examples in the following box, the reader would not know whether it was the committee, the department, the site or the whole organization that has problems or concerns.

> Our problems stem from the introduction of flexitime.
> Our concerns centre around the announcement of redundancies.

Other related problems come with phrases like 'in this area' (which area?) or 'next year' (calendar, academic or financial?).

How do I avoid an inappropriate tone and words?

Minutes must be written from a neutral position, representing the discussion in terms of what was discussed (rather than the style or manner of discussion). Beware of latching on to words that are said in the meeting and then using them. You are likely to follow the clearest speakers (or those you agree with) and the minutes will almost certainly be biased. Listen for the point of view and note this in your own words – minuting is a skill involving interpretation, not fast writing. Avoid words which describe the discussion and will be subjective. These include describing discussion as lively, heated, brief, lengthy, at length, etc.

What is a confidential minute?

In general, minutes are freely available to be read so if there is an item which would be inappropriate for others to see, you will need to create a 'confidential minute'. The chairperson should specifically ask the minute-taker to do this but you may feel it appropriate to ask for guidance in the meeting.

This should be a separate document, headed in the same way as the main minutes but titled 'confidential minute' and should again list those who were there. Type the minutes in the same style and format as the main set, using the appropriate number. In the main set of minutes, show the item number but just type 'confidential item' under the item heading.

Useful words for minutes

Although an accurate overview of the discussion should lead the minute-taker to the words that are necessary, there are occasions when it seems that the same word is used over and over again. In many cases this is the result of writing script-style minutes (the 'he said, she said' type), and simply removing the 'he said, she said' will reduce the problem.

The following are loosely grouped in no particular order. They cannot be used as synonyms; instead think of what you are trying to say and find the nearest alternative:

- discussed/debated/deliberated/considered/examined/analysed;
- said/stated/reported/established/confirmed/verified/declared;
- pointed out/explained/suggested/drew attention to/raised/ informed/understood;
- were reminded that/recalled/clarified/illustrated/defined/ demonstrated/emphasized;
- agreed/concurred;
- disagreed/disputed/not the case;
- planned/intended/meant/hoped/proposed;
- existence of/issue of/reality of/topic of/problem of/question of;
- benefits of/merits of/advantages of/worth/value of;
- problems/drawbacks/dangers/uncertainty/disadvantages;
- chose/opted/selected/picked/named/preferred;
- potential/possibility/likelihood/prospect/chance/probability;
- options/alternatives/choice/preference/opportunity;
- decided/resolved/approved/concluded/determined;
- worried/concerned/troubled/uneasy/anxious/apprehensive.

SUMMARY POINTS

- Take each item of the agenda in isolation and type it up according to good practice.
- Do not name names.
- Be consistent in style and depth.
- Make sure the minutes show who was there (and who was not), approval of previous minutes, updates on all past actions, and decisions and resulting actions.

12 Recording decisons and actions

A significant reason for having minutes is to provide an audit trail and, particularly in the public sector, this is taken increasingly seriously. The actions have to be presented in a way which is clear to the outsider and trackable through subsequent minutes (via 'Matters arising', or a more modern heading such as 'Update on actions').

Sometimes, there are areas where individual group members are unsure of what was discussed and rely on the minutes for an explanation. In many cases, people rely on the minutes to remind, if not inform, them of the actions they agreed to!

Noting the outcome of discussions does not sound particularly difficult. However, many groups conclude discussion with phrases like 'Right, we'll go with that' or 'Margot, you can take that forward' and the minute-taker is left unsure of what is going to happen.

It is essential that you leave the meeting knowing exactly who is doing what to make the group's decision a reality – the action triangle.

The action triangle

There are three aspects of an action point (see Figure 12.1):

What? Who?

When?

FIGURE 12.1 The action triangle

- precisely what is going to be done;
- who will take responsibility;
- when the action should be completed.

The 'who' must always be a member of the group. If actions are allocated to someone outside the group, there is no line of responsibility or mechanism for feedback. The committee member might do no more than give an instruction to someone, but the responsibility still lies within the group.

An example

Consider this unusually clear summary of the outcomes of a discussion on security given by the chairperson: 'Right, so we're agreed that Reception will not allow anyone in after 5.00 from 2 October. Chris, you'll sort it?' The minute-taker wrote the following:

Reception not to allow anyone in after 5.00 pm.

<div align="right">

Chris Francis

2 October 2017

</div>

This is not quite accurate as Reception's system needs to change from 2 October (not the deadline for Chris to take the action) and there is no clear link between Chris and Reception.

When clarifying the action in your mind, it is best to start with 'who?'

Answer: Chris.

Then ask what is he doing?

Answer: telling Reception not to allow anyone in after 5.00 pm from 2 October.

Finally, when is that person doing that action?

Answer: we don't know, no one said how much notice they would need.

The minute-taker should have interrupted to ask, 'When will that need to be done by?' Or, 'How much notice will they need?' It is possible to ask Chris, 'When will you do that?' However, in reality this sounds too much like taking over the job of the chairperson. Once the minute-taker knows the date, the action becomes:

Reception to be told not to allow anyone in after 5.00 pm from 2 October.

Chris Francis
25 September 2017

If you are not sure of any aspect of the action (or side of the triangle), you must ask. Interrupt with questions like:

- 'Please could you confirm the action for the minutes?'
- 'Could you give me a precise action for the minutes?'
- 'Please could you define the action for the minutes?'
- 'Who is responsible for that?'
- 'Whose action is that?'
- 'What is the deadline?'
- 'When is that to be completed?'

In fact these are some of the easiest interruptions to make because they are so factual. When you interrupt to ask, you will often find that others don't know either.

The deadline for many actions is just 'next time' or 'for the next meeting'. These need to be interpreted depending on what the action is, as some things will be needed for the agenda.

An example

'Seren, could you bring the model to the next meeting and we'll consider the fire escapes properly.' The deadline for this would be the date of the meeting.

'Alex, could you get the figures together and we'll look at them next time.' The deadline for this would be the deadline for agenda items because the figures should go out with the agenda.

Many deadlines are given casually: 'I'm seeing her on Wednesday, I'll have a chat then', would be minuted as:

Nerys Welch to be asked to canvas her team about their willingness to provide cover over the Christmas period.

Steve King
10 May 2017

When they decide to do nothing

This is a positive outcome, but it will be a decision with no action. Make sure to differentiate between deciding to do nothing, and not deciding anything.

An example

Online training: The committee agreed that the company's online training was generally of good quality but would need to be updated to reflect the office upgrade. As the upgrade comes with its own training package, it was decided not to invest further in the in-house system.

When there is no outcome

Ideally each minute should be 'closed', that is, a confirmation of how the discussion ended. Although it may be obvious now, this will make the minutes clearer for future readers. This is usually an action point, but often there is nothing more to be done or the group did not or could not reach agreement.

If the group agreed there was no need for them to take any action, replace the action with 'No action necessary', using the same layout as the action points. This will usually follow items for discussion only (although sometimes these will result in an action).

If the group did not get as far as taking an action (when one was required), the term is 'No decision taken' or 'No decision made'. You will probably need to ask the chairperson whether to put it on the agenda for a future meeting.

If the group were arguing and could not reach a decision, use 'No consensus reached'. Again, ask whether to include the item on the next agenda.

If it was agreed to discuss the item at a future meeting, the phrasing is 'Deferred to next meeting' or 'Deferred to meeting on [date]'. If the item had to be passed to another group, the action point should be replaced with 'Referred to…'. This latter alternative is likely also to have a reason; for example 'Referred to Health and Safety Committee for advice' or 'Referred to Board for approval'.

Layout of action points

Most people do not read minutes in any great depth. Most just skim them and many just look for their action points. These readers are likely to miss actions that are buried within a paragraph, so the action must be a separate paragraph, even if it is just a few words.

In terms of the layout, there are many ways of presenting an action in minutes. The clearest is an action column, but anything that achieves the aim of clear presentation is acceptable. All the

variations in Figure 12.2 would be a separate paragraph and usually indented from the left margin. The first is clearest, followed by the final version. Avoid typing the action point in bold as it is likely to be followed by a heading, also in bold, and the action will be visually tied to the wrong heading.

The team decided that the Christmas party would be open to all staff and their partners. There would be no charge for staff members but partners would be asked to contribute £38 to cover food and wine at the table. | **Sue Taylor**
Details to be included in November e-news | 20 May 2017

The team decided that the Christmas party would be open to all staff and their partners. There would be no charge for staff members but partners would be asked to contribute £38 to cover food and wine at the table.
Details to be included in November e-news
Sue Taylor *(20 May 2017)*

The team decided that the Christmas party would be open to all staff and their partners. There would be no charge for staff members but partners would be asked to contribute £38 to cover food and wine at the table.
Sue Taylor *to submit details for inclusion in November e-news (20 May 2017)*

The team decided that the Christmas party would be open to all staff and their partners. There would be no charge for staff members but partners would be asked to contribute £38 to cover food and wine at the table.
ACTION: *Details to be included in November e-news*
Sue Taylor *(20 May 2017)*

The team decided that the Christmas party would be open to all staff and their partners. There would be no charge for staff members but partners would be asked to contribute £38 to cover food and wine at the table.
Details to be included in November e-news **Sue Taylor**
20 May 2017

FIGURE 12.2 Example layouts for action points

When there are several actions for one minute

Where possible the minute should be split with subheadings and the resulting action in the appropriate place. This is not always possible, usually because the actions are so interwoven that they cannot be split, but different people may take on aspects of the action. Where this happens, show each aspect of the action separately with the name and deadline. Example layouts are shown as Figure 12.3.

Managing an action log

An action log is different to action minutes. Action minutes are a list of actions from a meeting, sometimes showing the decision as well. An action log is a rolling list of actions with updates until the point where they are completed or abandoned, at which point they remain as hidden text or are moved to a separate log for filing.

An action log provides an easy-to-use record of the status of actions and, for that reason, is often preferred by meeting attendees and chairpersons. However, they also bring problems in their use:

- they make extra work for the minute-taker as they have to be managed in addition to the minutes;
- they are often poorly designed as a heavily lined table and insufficient cell margins to make the text visually clear;
- a lot of paper is wasted, particularly where there are a series of updates for one item which leaves several empty columns;
- the management of the log becomes an administrative task and tends to be removed from the management of the group.

The team decided that the party would be held at The Rainbow and be open to all staff and their partners. There would be no charge for staff members but partners would be asked to contribute £38 to cover food and wine at the table.

Provisional booking to be made at The Rainbow	**Ami Chi**
for 120 people on 1 September	2 June 2017
Details to be included in July e-news	**Sue Taylor**
	30 June 2017

The team decided that the Christmas party would be held at The Rainbow and be open to all staff and their partners. There would be no charge for staff members but partners would be asked to contribute £38 to cover food and wine at the table.

Provisional booking to be made at The Rainbow for 120 people
***Ami Chi** (2 June 2017)*
Details to be included in July e-news
***Sue Taylor** (30 June 2017)*

The team decided that the Christmas party would be held at The Rainbow and be open to all staff and their partners. There would be no charge for staff members but partners would be asked to contribute £38 to cover food and wine at the table.

***Ami Chi** to make provisional booking at The Rainbow for 120 people on 1 September (2 June 2017)*
***Sue Taylor** to submit details for inclusion in July e-news (30 June 2017)*

The team decided that the Christmas party would be held at The Rainbow and be open to all staff and their partners. There would be no charge for staff members but partners would be asked to contribute £38 to cover food and wine at the table.

ACTION: Provisional booking to be made at The Rainbow for 120 people on 1 September
***Ami Chi** (2 June 2017)*
Details to be included in July e-news
***Sue Taylor** (30 June 2017)*

The team decided that the Christmas party would be held at The Rainbow and be open to all staff and their partners. There would be no charge for staff members but partners would be asked to contribute £38 to cover food and wine at the table.

Provisional booking to be made at The Rainbow	**Ami Chi**
for 120 people on 1 September	2 June 2017
Details to be included in July e-news	**Sue Taylor**
	30 June 2017

FIGURE 12.3 Example layouts for multiple actions

RAG or traffic-light systems

Some groups use a colour-coded system to support the log. This is often called a RAG or traffic-light system because the colours red, amber and green are used. Different organizations, or different meetings within one organization, can use this system in different ways so it is important to be clear what is meant by each colour.

Used badly, this system can result in colour overload and of course is little use in the case of colour blindness or use of monotone printers. It is better to have a 'key' column where just a small box is coloured.

To make an action log work

The actions must be completely clear and stand alone – define exactly what the person has to do, name them and give a deadline. (See Figure 12.4.)

Each action remains on the log until it can be shown as 'completed'. It remains on the log for the next meeting (so the group know it is completed), and then can be removed to be filed separately. The filing system must enable an outsider to link discussion, decision, action and action management in the event of future questions.

If it becomes impossible to complete an action, this should be shown as 'abandoned', or something similar, together with a reason.

Where actions are ongoing, there should be dated updates with new deadlines. Again, they must be clear to an outsider in the future. Updates must appear with the original action, not at various places throughout the log. It should be possible to read from the beginning to end of the action in one place.

The log must be cross-referenced to the minutes so it is easy to find out more about the discussion if needed.

It must be clear from the minutes that the group knew that an action was completed and, perhaps more importantly, knew when

Date, 2017	Action	Responsibility
23 March Item 5.2	**Format** A list of aspects of achievement to be drawn up and circulated to the group for amendment and suggestions. 24/3/17 ***Action abandoned due to short timescale***	Yvonne McKillian 14 April 2017
Item 5.3	**Venue** The quote of £32/head from Weston Grange to be accepted. Holiday Inn and Hilton to be thanked and the reservations released. 24/3/17 ***Completed***	Alan Turner 24 March 2017
Item 7.1	**Publicity** Local/business press, radio and TV stations within [area] to be telephoned with invitation to the lunch and offer of interviews. To be followed up with written details. 21/4/17 Initial telephone contact made with 14 newspapers and 5 radio/TV stations and written details sent. Two papers will cover the event, remainder to be chased up by e-mail 19/5/17 Further two responses received including one from local television. County newspaper and local radio to be telephoned the week before the lunch to encourage attendance. 9/6/17 ***Completed***	Adam Davey 21 April 2017 Adam Davey 19 May 2017 Adam Davey 1 June 2017

FIGURE 12.4 Example action log

it hadn't been and what would happen as a result. It is not enough to minute, 'The group reviewed the action log.' You must minute which actions have been completed and demonstrate that the group knew and accepted what was happening about the others. Where an action is abandoned it must be with the group's knowledge and acceptance.

Give serious thought to the design. The default layout for a table does not usually support practical use – the lines are too heavy,

the vertical cell margins are non-existent and text has to be small to fit into the table. Make sure the lines are grey and the columns are a sensible width according to the content. Don't waste a column on repeated text (eg the date of the meeting).

Remember that just like the 'Matters arising' on minutes, the action log is there to enable the group to manage the actions that are being undertaken on their behalf, and to create an audit trail in the event of problems in the future.

SUMMARY POINTS

- Action is made up of three parts, *who* is doing *what* (precisely) by *when*.
- The action must be the responsibility of a member of the group.
- Make it clear if there is a decision to do nothing.
- If an action log is used, make sure it is clear whether the group knew that actions had been completed and, if not, what was to be done next.

13 Layout and numbering

Layout

The way you lay out your minutes is important. A good layout will encourage your readers to pick up the minutes because they will look accessible. The reader will be guided smoothly forwards so they keep reading and they will better understand the contents. It will also influence the perception of the actual quality of the minutes: if they look untidy and muddled, the reader is likely to assume the content is equally poor. In addition, there are the concerns about writing to support dyslexia, but good practice for that is also generally good practice for the non-dyslexic reader.

The layout for minutes broadly follows the layout for a report but with the important addition of clear decisions and action points.

Page layout

Minutes can be blocked or indented. Blocked is slightly quicker and easier to type, and may save a few lines (see Figure 13.1).

6. **Holiday camps, Summer 2017**
 All the schools that were approached offered the necessary
 accommodation and facilities but some were priced too highly.
 It was agreed to proceed with Manor Park School (weeks 1–2),
 Tolbridge Girls School (weeks 3–5) and Amering Hall (week 6).
 Confirm bookings with schools above **David Markess**
 13 October 2016

7. **Family placements**

7.1. Family placement with Mrs Bryant
 Mrs Bryant owns a group of holiday cottages and has offered
 a cottage for one week, during term time, during April or May
 2017 to a family of up to six. It was agreed to ask a volunteer
 to visit her and, assuming she wishes to proceed, to take up her
 offer and agree a suitable date.
 Member of voluntary administration team to visit
 Mrs Bryant **Adam Turner**
 20 October 2016

7.2 The possibility of extending the scheme to family placements was
 discussed and it was agreed to consider this following the first
 placement.
 Extending the scheme to be discussed at the
 October 2016 meeting **Sarah Kaminski**
 25 October 2016

FIGURE 13.1 Example of blocked layout

Indented is the more commonly preferred style because it is easier
to read and the layout reinforces the relative importance of the
information (see Figure 13.2).

Text should not be justified (set out with straight left and right
margins), as this is often harder to read because of the 'stretching'
of the spaces to meet the margin. Justified text is often a significant
barrier for readers with dyslexia, and the minutes are less effective
to the extent that a few are unable to read documents in that
format. Minutes with a 'ragged' right margin are easier to read.

6. **Holiday camps, Summer 2017**

 All the schools that were approached offered the necessary accommodation and facilities but some were priced too highly. It was agreed to proceed with Manor Park School (weeks 1–2), Tolbridge Girls School (weeks 3–5) and Amering Hall (week 6).
 Confirm bookings with schools above
 Action: **David Markess** 13 October 2016

7. **Family placement**

 7.1 **Family placement with Mrs Bryant**
 Mrs Bryant owns a group of holiday cottages and has offered a cottage for one week, during term-time, during April or May 2017 to a family of up to six. It was agreed to ask a volunteer to visit her and, assuming she wishes to proceed, to take up her offer and agree a suitable date.
 Member of voluntary administration team to visit Mrs Bryant
 Action: **Adam Turner** 20 October 2016

 7.2 The possibility of extending the scheme to family placements was discussed and it was agreed to consider this following the first placement.
 Extending the scheme to be discussed at the October 2016 meeting
 Action: **Sarah Kaminski** 25 October 2016

FIGURE 13.2 Example of indented layout

USING AN ACTION COLUMN

An action column is the easiest style to read, but few minute-takers use it because of the difficulty caused in typing. It is generally set up in a table in order to get the column but this causes problems in lining up the actions against the text, particularly if frequent edits are made.

An action column is the easiest style to read for minutes because the reader can skim through, looking for their name. It is generally set up in a table with the borders blanked out except for the action

column line. It is easiest to set up a new table for every minute item to avoid problems lining up the action name/date with the text, or as the table goes over a page. If your readers will read it as a Word document, it is better to make the borders white (rather than blanked out) so they do not show.

Always show the action text as a new paragraph with the name and deadline date in the right column.

USING AN ACTION BOX

If there are few actions, it may not be worth wasting the space of a column throughout the document. Prepare an action box: a table of one row and three columns. Type the heading 'Action' in the first column, set up the second for the text to align to the top of the cell and the third to align to the bottom. If your normal font size is 12, you might want to make the third column eleven or ten-point and then type the name in bold. This layout is shown in Figure 13.3 with the frame shown in grey to illustrate the layout. When using this layout, the lines should be white/uncoloured except for the action column line. Set up a master action box which can be cut and pasted wherever an action is typed.

Action:	The 'what' part of the action should be typed here, aligned to the top of the cell.	
		Name and date typed here, aligned to bottom of cell.

FIGURE 13.3 Text box layout

Typing minutes as a table

Minutes are often typed as a table. This makes it particularly easy to spot decisions and actions (which are often all that people want to read) but does tend to take up more space. The default layouts for tables are far from reader-friendly, with the darkness of the lines fighting the text for the reader's attention and the text squashed into each cell. It is well worth preparing a good master template which can then be used for subsequent minutes.

To improve the layout of the table:

- Use borders and shading to change the line colour from black to grey.

- In the 'Page Layout' tab, use cell margins to give a larger top and bottom margin (the default is zero). Generally a top margin of 0.15 and a bottom margin of 0.1 suits most tables.

See Figure 13.4 for examples of good and bad practice.

Poor layout	Black lines for table
Zero top margin	Zero bottom margin

Good layout	Grey lines for table
0.15 top margin	0.1 bottom margin

FIGURE 13.4 Good and bad practice for the layout of tables

Headings

The layout of headings should represent their relative importance. So, for example, the heading of item 9 is larger than the heading of item 9.1.

FIGURE 13.5 Example text sizing

Assuming 12-point text, headings should be 13- or 14-point bold. The most common style for professional-looking minutes is shown as Figure 13.5.

Typing rules

All the usual rules of typing, summarized below, apply to minutes:

One space	between words
Two spaces	after a full stop, exclamation mark or question mark (between sentences)
One blank line	between paragraphs after a heading
Two blank lines	between sections

Layout for 'Present', etc

If you have not numbered 'Apologies' on the agenda, it can be included with the other names in columns at the start of the minutes. If you prefer to number it, leave it as number 1 in the minutes and omit it from the names at the start of the minutes.

Simple numbering

It is a convention of minutes that the numbering and heading on the agenda are carried over to the minutes. The two exceptions are 'Apologies', which broadens out to 'Present', and where an objective is numbered on the agenda and so is reworded as a heading on the minutes.

Most minutes are numbered from '1' for each meeting. This is probably the simplest method, and if reference is made to old minutes it can be done as 4.3/7.17 (item 4.3 of the July 2017 meeting).

Continuous numbering

If items are frequently carried forward, you might want to give an item a number that it will keep throughout its life. This system usually reverts to '1' for the first item of the first meeting each year. Again, items from a previous year can be referenced as 258/17 (item 258 in 2017).

If you use this system, consideration should be given as to whether the administrative items (minutes of previous meeting, matters arising) should be numbered or whether you should leave them blank and just number the information/discussion/decision items. If you leave them unnumbered, do the same for 'Any other business' and then continue the minutes' numbers to those items when they are typed up.

As the agenda headings and numbering form the basis for the minutes, it is worth giving some thought to the numbering at the early stages of the meeting.

Numbering for subheadings

The simplest system is to use the standard report style, illustrated in Figure 13.6.

6. Heading

6.1 Subheading

(a) **Sub-subheading**

FIGURE 13.6 Example three-level numbering

6. Heading

6.1 Subheading

6.1.1 Sub-subheading

(a) **Sub-sub-subheading**

FIGURE 13.7 Example four-level numbering

If you need to use a fourth level of numbering for an item, this can be done as illustrated in Figure 13.7. If this is necessary for any item in the minutes, it should be done throughout. For example, if item 9 needs a fourth level of numbering, the third level will be '9.1.1'. The third level of all items should then be 'X.1.1' even if there is no fourth level.

Look at the picture

Before you dispatch the minutes, look at them from too far away to read. Do they look professional and invite the reader to read? Are the headings consistently sized? Can the actions be quickly spotted?

SUMMARY POINTS

- Look at your minutes page by page to check consistency of layout.
- Use left-aligned text.
- Scale the headings to reflect their importance.
- Make sure that actions are easy to spot.

14 Minutes for different types of meeting

The broad rules and principles apply to all types of meeting, but their application varies. Most of this book has focused on business-type meetings, those with a group who meet regularly, but there are differences in the way the minutes are presented for:

- HR meetings (disciplinary or grievance).
- Investigatory meetings.
- Multi-disciplinary meetings.
- Social care meetings.
- One-off meetings.
- Negotiation meetings.

HR meetings

Meetings within human resources are likely to be concerning a grievance or a disciplinary. The minutes are taken as a record for the employer. They should show the case being made, the response to that case, any questions and the response that these elicit. There is likely to be a subsequent panel discussion to be minuted together with the outcome.

They do not have to be shown to the person with a grievance or under the disciplinary process but it is likely to show the employer in a poor light if they are not shared.

It is important that the minute-taker interrupts if there is a problem in understanding or keeping up. To ask someone afterwards risks an unreliable memory or individual bias (even manipulation) and there is no 'next meeting' where corrections can be made by the group. Although it is uncomfortable to interrupt it gives confidence to all parties that the notes are being well taken as issues are clarified as they happen. It is perfectly acceptable for the minute-taker to say, 'As I understand it, XYZ – is that correct for the minutes?'

The minutes are the ultimate responsibility of the person who ran the meeting and the draft should be typed-up immediately and passed to that person for checking.

Once the minutes are circulated, changes cannot be made by any one party so any requested amendments should be shown as a post-meeting note or an addendum.

Structure of the meeting

The meeting may not have a formal agenda, but it should have a clear, planned structure (an agenda can be provided if required and the process must be explained by the chairperson at the start).

WELCOME AND INTRODUCTIONS

This usually involves the chairperson calling the meeting to order. The names of those attending and any who have sent apologies are given/confirmed.

PURPOSE AND PROCESS

The purpose of the meeting should be stated. The chair should outline the process that will be followed, when questions will be allowed, etc.

SITUATION / CURRENT POSITION / PRESENTATIONS

For an investigation or disciplinary meeting, the person 'making the case' will explain the situation and answer questions; the person under investigation will then have the opportunity to question, comment and state their case. That person can then be questioned. A grievance meeting should follow the same principle, but the person with the grievance will start by explaining it and the manager or employer will answer it. For both types of meeting, witnesses may be called in for comment or to produce paper documents to support a case. The chairperson should summarize and guide throughout. A final opportunity for questions or comments should be given. It may be appropriate for each party to summarize their argument before the close. The chairperson should then close this stage of the meeting while the panel make their decision.

PANEL DISCUSSION

This will not necessarily happen for every panel meeting. The panel will discuss the merits of the various arguments they have heard and make their decision. Although this is minuted, it is unlikely to be made generally available.

DECISION/OUTCOME

This is the statement of the decision made and the formal reason for it. It is likely to include next action or actions to be taken as a result of the meeting and may state the process for follow-up or future meeting.

The agenda

A panel meeting may have an agenda or it may be that there is a *chairperson's brief*, available to the chair and minute-taker. This is broadly the same as an agenda, listing the people involved, purpose,

Disciplinary meeting: Mr Jonathan Turner
12 January 2017, 9.30 am
Committee Room 1, Capstone Building

Welcome and introductions

Chair:	Nigel Barnes, Asst Director HR
Invited:	Jonathan Turner, Financial Analyst
	Mary Dean, HR Manager, Investigating Officer
	Damian Brookes, HR Staff Support
Minutes:	Alex Brodie, HR Administrator

Purpose and process

This meeting has been called in response to concerns about Mr Turner's timekeeping and attendance over the first three months of 2017.

Marion Daneski

Jonathan Turner

General comments and questions

The meeting will adjourn for panel discussion

Decision/outcome

The outcome will be advised in writing within 24 hours.

Papers
- *Timesheets, clock-in records*
- *Witness statement: Steven Marks, Finance Manager*

FIGURE 14.1 Agenda for disciplinary meeting

structure, timings and other reminders. If an agenda is not to be circulated, it is useful to advise members prior to the meeting of the process that will be followed or it is essential that the process is outlined at the start.

List the people who will be attending, using full names to help the participants refer to each other correctly. It is useful to note roles, job title, and/or employing organization as appropriate (see Figure 14.1). The heading 'Agenda' is not generally used.

PAPERS

There are likely to be papers and other supporting documents and these should be circulated to members before the meeting. They must be clearly referenced and numbered (pages, sections and possibly even paragraphs) so that the panel can find relevant information

quickly. It may be helpful to provide ring binders to keep everything in order.

CONSULTATION

It is essential that the chair and minute-taker consult before the meeting so the minute-taker knows exactly what is going on, what is expected and can prepare some parts of the minutes before the meeting (eg the statement of purpose, process). All papers should be available to the minute-taker.

Taking notes

Although the minutes are likely to follow the discussion in a business meeting, they are not meant to be a transcript. They should record the points made but not the words used to make those points. It is important to demonstrate that due process was followed; so, for example, if a meeting is adjourned when someone gets upset, this should be noted on the lines of, 'Julie became upset and the meeting was adjourned for five minutes.' Or, 'David confirmed that he was happy for the meeting to continue without a union representative.' Do not minute it as, 'Sara Jackson, David's union representative, was held up in traffic. Lisa asked David whether he wanted to defer the meeting or continue and David confirmed that he was happy for the meeting to go ahead without Sara.'

The minutes

WELCOME AND INTRODUCTIONS

List those who attended, showing organization, department or job title as appropriate. This is usually done under the heading of 'Attended'. If there are any apologies, these should also be shown; anyone who doesn't turn up is listed under 'Invited, but did not attend'. Leave a small space before typing your name under 'Minutes' or 'Note-taker' to show that you were not part of the panel. If you combine a role in the panel with note-taking, don't insert the space.

PURPOSE

This should summarize the purpose of the meeting as given by the chairperson, and can usually be entered into the minutes before the meeting.

PROCESS

Although it is not essential to minute the chairperson's explanation of the process, it may be relevant to show this to demonstrate that due process was followed.

THE MEETING

The relevant points should be summarized. Although panel minutes generally follow the structure of what was said at the meeting, it is important that they do not become a transcript (see Figure 14.2).

Poor practice	Good practice
GM So Tina, it is clear that you are consistently 10–15 minutes late each morning.	Tina accepted that she is regularly late and explained that, following a change to the bus times, she is unable to drop her son at school and get a bus in time for a 9.00 am start.
TM Yes, it's because the bus times have changed. I've explained it all to Sally… there is nothing I can do about it.	
DS Why can't you get an earlier bus?	
TM I have to drop my little boy at school and they don't open until 8.40.	
GM Can a neighbour or friend not take him?	
TM There's no one who lives near me.	
VG So why has this suddenly become a problem?	
TM The first year was fine because the bus left at 8.45 and I could just get here on time, but now it leaves at 8.35 and the next one is 8.55.	
GM Could you drop your son off a little earlier?	
TM We're not allowed to – the gates are locked and I'm not going to leave him standing on the street while I get on a bus and drive away.	
VG Could you not walk down to the main road and the other buses?	
TM Ever since I fell in the snow, I can't walk far or fast, my knee is too sore.	

FIGURE 14.2 Poor practice and good practice

PANEL DISCUSSION

The key points made should be minuted. They should be written up so they make sense as a document, not necessarily following the order of the discussion (which is likely to be all over the place!) (see Figure 14.3).

'Tina's good, she works hard and fits in well with the team' 'She seemed quite stroppy' 'She's under a lot of pressure, she's gone from wife with part time job in happy families situation to full-time responsibility for all of it… she didn't see it coming' 'She'd struggle to get another job like the one she's got here' 'But we can't just keep her in County Hall as a one-woman satellite accounts department' 'If we give in to her, everyone will want to stay here' 'Not quite everyone!' 'But we should do what we can to keep her – she's good and we've invested quite a bit in her training so far' *General agreement*	The panel considered Tina's case and agreed they would like her to remain within the accounts department.

FIGURE 14.3 Example summary of discussion

DECISION/OUTCOME

Minute a clear statement of the decision and any actions that arise from it.

DATE OF NEXT MEETING/REVIEW

This is not necessarily needed, but if some follow-up is planned include it with an appropriate heading.

CORRECTIONS TO MINUTES

Whereas changes to business minutes can be made at the next meeting, this is not usually the case for panel meetings. It is therefore best to include a statement along the lines of:

Any amendments to the minutes to be notified to [name/e-mail] by [date]. The minutes will then be deemed an accurate record.

If any changes are made, they should be included as an addendum or post-meeting note but the minutes should not be changed.

Preparation

A lot of the minutes can be pre-prepared: the names, purpose and process (in consultation with the chairperson) and the case being made by the employer (from HR notes). It is important to listen carefully in the meeting to ensure that when the case is made it is the same as was in the notes – you will need to amend what you've prepared if it differs.

Case conferences / best-interest or multi-disciplinary meetings

These are the meetings held to discuss the current or future care of a sick or vulnerable person. They may comprise staff from one organization or can bring together people from a range of organizations or locations.

Although a typical structure is listed below, it is essential that the minute-taker is properly briefed about the case, the current situation and who will be involved. Guidance should also be given about what is needed from the minutes and the chairperson should guide the minute-taker as appropriate during the meeting.

Structure

A typical case conference will start in the same way as a grievance/ disciplinary with introductions, purpose and process. From there it can follow one of two possible structures:

DISCIPLINE-BASED

For example, each discipline will comment from their involvement with the vulnerable person. This may include clinical staff, social services, education, police, etc. The minute-taker should summarize the input of each. This can take the form of an ordinary summary or bullet points under each heading. The minutes should include updates on previous actions, current situation and future actions as appropriate.

SERVICE-USER CENTRED

This focuses on the service-user's situations and includes the input of the professionals at each stage. For example, a young person's behaviour at school, medical condition, involvement with police, communication with social worker. Although the relevant professional is likely to have the greatest input at each stage, all there discuss each aspect. Again there should be monitoring of past actions and definition of future ones. The discussion should be minuted as subject-based, not speech-based. So record that, 'The police are aware of increased drug use on the estate', not, 'PC Eunson reported an increase of drug use on the the estate.'

Although it will be necessary to use some names, many can be removed, which will result in clearer minutes that are about the service user, not the professionals. For example:

Replace: PC Eunson reported that the police are aware of increased drug use on the estate.

With: The police are aware of increased drug use on the estate.

Replace: Mary Jones said that she had visited the family on four occasions but was told Marcus was out, playing with friends.

With: Mary Jones visited the family on four occasions but was told Marcus was out, playing with friends.

Replace: Dr Singh explained that he had used [drug] in a similar case with excellent results.

With: Dr Singh has used [drug] in a similar case with excellent results.

Where someone gives lengthy information, avoid prefacing each paragraph with 'Sarah explained', 'Sarah added', 'Sarah outlined', etc. This can be done by changing the heading to read 'Social Worker's Report (Sarah Burns)' and then listing the points made as paragraphs or bullet points.

It is often helpful to produce a summary of actions, included at the end of the minutes or sent as a separate document.

Team or open meetings

The key difference in these types of meetings is that it is not such a tightly defined group who attend, they are usually for those who are in the workplace on the day, or (for open meetings) who want to attend.

The minutes of most meetings are broadly the same in terms of structure and the purpose of the minutes remains the same. There are, however, a few differences, usually in terms of the style of the minutes.

The team meeting

If the meeting is quite formal and well-structured with participants expected to attend, the minutes should follow the good practice outlined throughout the book. If the meeting is more casual and

attended by those who are in the workplace that day, there are a few changes:

- The language is often less formal; for example using *isn't* instead of *is not*.
- The job titles are often not shown but it is worth considering whether it would be useful for future readers to show these.
- Those who were there are listed under 'Attended'; and 'Apologies' for those who advised of non-attendance.
- 'Absent' is not used for those who didn't turn up.

Make sure that relative informality doesn't result in failure to approve the minutes and check up on the actions. The audit trail is just as important at this level so actions need to be clearly defined and trackable through Matters Arising (although you might prefer a less formal heading such as Update on Actions).

The open meeting

The heading 'attended' is usually used to show those who were there, and 'apologies' is only used if anyone specifically advised of their non-attendance.

The language is likely to be more formal than a team meeting but otherwise the discussion is minuted following the good practice outlined throughout the book.

The one-off or ad hoc meeting

These are usually held in response to a situation and often with little notice. Formal minutes may not be required, or appropriate, but you may be asked to 'take notes' (with little guidance as to what this actually means).

As with a regular meeting, start with a list of names, but this is under the heading of 'Attended' rather than 'Present'. You are

unlikely to need 'In attendance' but may need 'Apologies'. Anyone who didn't turn up should be listed under 'Invited, but did not attend'.

The first paragraph should be an outline of the issue that's necessitated the meeting, usually under a relevant heading.

If a bit of detail is required, summarize the reason for the decision and the decision itself in the second paragraph (the word 'Outcome' may be more appropriate than 'Decision'). For many meetings it will be enough just to list the outcome/decision.

The action should be the final paragraph – a clear definition of *who* is doing *what* by *when*.

An e-mail 'note of the meeting'

Meeting notes are often combined with an e-mail. In this situation:

- 'Attended' is replaced with the names in the 'To' box (so ensure a complete list in alphabetic order).
- The name of the meeting is replaced with the subject line (so ensure it is descriptive and relevant).
- The content will be the same as the paragraphs outlined above.

Make sure there is a system in place so that the completion of the action is recorded, either by asking for a 'reply all' from the person responsible or through an appropriate filing system.

The negotiation meeting

These often involve buyers and suppliers or trade unions and management. The participants should be listed in the same way as the one-off meeting, but there may then be several subjects discussed; each should have a separate heading and they should be in a logical order, irrespective of when the points were raised. There

may be occasions when names will be necessary but this should be avoided as far as possible:

Replace: Charles Heaton requested that letterhead be a minimum weight of 80 g with a good density. Sukira Ahmed said that this was not possible within the budget unless a minimum order of £10,000 was given.

With: The Trust require that the letterhead is 80 g with good density. Alpha Stationery can provide this if a minimum order of £10,000 is given.

Video/audio conferencing

These meetings are generally disliked by minute-takers, usually because of the difficulties of knowing who is speaking and hearing what is said. Once a minute-taker is aware of the need to minute what is discussed rather than what individuals say these problems are reduced.

As it is essential to get a name for an action, the minute-taker should interrupt if it is not clear who is responsible. A simple, 'Excuse me, who is that who's responsible for X?' should get the necessary name.

Make sure you know who is expected and ask the chairperson to arrange introductions. Actively listen to the voices, perhaps making notes of any specific traits to help you identify who is who (eg Andy = Scottish; Mary = echo on line).

If possible, ensure you are seated in the same room as the chairperson and have eye contact so you can quickly and quietly ask for information that's needed. Make sure that you have a clear idea of the agenda items and know where decisions are expected. If you miss one (or if it isn't made) you should interrupt and ask what is being done (eg 'Excuse me, what is the action for item 6?' or 'Excuse me, what is the decision on funding for X?').

Board meetings

In some ways a board meeting is easier to minute than an everyday one because, although they are more 'high powered', they are generally much more structured and formally run.

There is no standard level of detail or format for the minutes of board meetings. They should give enough information to demonstrate how the board came to their decision. They are usually formal in style, language and layout and the good practice outlined in this book is applicable throughout.

On some boards, particularly in the public sector, there are the 'governing body' who make decisions but also regularly attending managers/directors who give information and may join in the discussion. These managers or directors often have resulting actions and will be answerable for them at the next meeting. This presents a problem because they are not the decision-makers (so listed under 'Present'), but cannot be 'In Attendance' because they are answerable for their actions. The best way around this is to use the heading 'Present' but then list 'voting members' and 'other members'. The heading 'In attendance' can then be used for one-off attendees in the usual way.

In general, boards tend to have fewer actions, their purpose often being to approve or ratify reports or the decision of sub-committees or other groups. This means that the decision is often to 'approve', 'confirm', 'accept' or 'note' but with no resulting action.

Ensure that all papers that are submitted to the board have a consistent layout and all should have a cover sheet giving:

- the name of the board;
- the date of the meeting;
- the title of the paper, its author and any other administrative information;
- a one-paragraph summary;
- the recommendation(s), written in a form that is ready for approval.

The last two points can be copied direct to the minutes, saving the need for note-taking *in* the meeting. Where the papers will form part of the minutes, they will not usually need to be minuted. It is enough to say, 'The board received the finance report.'

However, many minutes are posted on the internet without the papers being available to readers, so it is necessary to give a summary. If the cover sheet includes a short summary, or, for a longer report, if an executive summary is produced, this should simply be copied into the minutes. If this is not provided, avoid the repetition of the reporting manager's name in each paragraph by bracketing the name in the heading then listing the points made underneath:

Finance Report (John Donaldson)

If a question is raised to simply clarify a point or misunderstanding, this should not be minuted. If genuine discussion arises, particularly if it results in an action, include this in the minutes. It should not be necessary to note who raised the point being discussed, although you might want to minute, 'The board queried how this would be financed', particularly to demonstrate the board's effectiveness at holding to account.

If there are public questions, these are usually headed with the subject raised and the name of the person who raised it. The questions should be summarized and then the answer should be given under a subheading of 'Response'.

Some board meetings still have 'proposers' and 'seconders' and a vote taken on decisions. In this case, the decisions should be recorded on the lines of:

- Rashif Rai proposed that the budget be cut by 4 per cent; seconded by Sarah Martin and carried by 10 votes to two.
- Motion: that the budget be cut by 4 per cent. Proposed by Rashif Rai, seconded by Sarah Martin; carried 10:2.

SUMMARY POINTS

- The basic principles of minute taking apply to all types of meetings, but their application differs.

- All minutes should show who attended and, depending on depth, information to explain why the outcomes were reached and the actions that will take them forward.

- There should always be a means of demonstrating to future readers whether actions were completed.

Creating Success Series

Dealing with Difficult People Roy Lilley
Decision Making and Problem Solving John Adair
Develop Your Leadership Skills John Adair
Develop Your Presentation Skills Theo Theobald
How to Manage People Michael Armstrong
How to Organize Yourself John Caunt
How to Write a Business Plan Brian Finch
How to Write a Marketing Plan John Westwood
How to Write Reports and Proposals Patrick Forsyth
Improve Your Communication Skills Alan Barker
Successful Project Management Trevor L Young
Successful Time Management Patrick Forsyth
Taking Minutes of Meetings Joanna Gutmann

The above titles are available from all good bookshops.

For further information on these and other Kogan Page titles, or to order online, visit the Kogan Page website at: **www.koganpage.com**.